1964

ther quiet . . .

was a good y
And Chris
went to the
we (my
nd it wa
es I receiv

The Story of
My Life (so far)

The Story of
My Life (so far)

CHARLES FORAN

HarperCollins*PublishersLtd*

First edition

*Lyrics to "King of the Road" by Roger Miller (© 1964 Sony/ATV Tree LLC. — renewed),
reprinted by permission. All rights reserved and administered by Sony/ATV Music Publishing,
8 Music Square West, Nashville, TN 37203.*

*Lyrics to "A Place to Stand" reprinted by permission of Gordon V. Thompson Music, a division
of Warner/Chappell Music Canada Ltd.*

Words from Green Eggs and Ham *by Dr. Seuss (TM and © 1960 and renewed 1988 by
Dr. Seuss Enterprises, L.P.), reprinted by permission of Random House, Inc.*

Words from Chicken Soup with Rice *by Maurice Sendak © 1962. Published by
HarperCollins Publishers.*

Words from Pierre *by Maurice Sendak © 1962. Published by HarperCollins Publishers.*

Words from An American Childhood *by Annie Dillard © 1987. Published by
HarperCollins Publishers.*

Canadian Cataloguing in Publication Data

Foran, Charles, 1960–
The story of my life (so far) : a happy childhood

ISBN 0-00-255441-0 (bound)
ISBN 0-00-638488-9 (pbk.)

1. Foran, Charles, 1960– —Childhood and youth. 2. Authors, Canadian
(English)—20th century—Biography.* I. Title.

PS8561.O633Z53 1998   C818'.5409   C98-931103-1
PR9199.3.F67Z472 1998

98 99 00 01 02 03 04 HC 10 9 8 7 6 5 4 3 2 1

Printed and bound in the United States

I woke in bits, like all children, piecemeal over the years . . . I noticed this process of waking, and predicted with terrifying logic that one of these years not far away I would be awake continuously and never slip back, and never be free of myself again.

Annie Dillard,
An American Childhood

for Debbie and the boys

Contents

1965

I'm God's son, I say.

George doesn't answer.

Mary Virgin and Joseph Carpenter were put on earth to have God's babies. He is our dad. We're his kids.

He thinks for a second. How many children does God have? he asks.

Lots.

My mom looks after four every day.

God has more than that, I reply, pretty sure about this. Way more.

Estelle Avenue is empty. Only a few cars zoom past. It's kind of lonely out here. Kind of scary. Finch Avenue Public, where hard boys go, isn't even open yet. Light bounces off windows. A flag sleeps on its pole. I kick stones and pop cans. George tries to whistle.

You can't whistle, I say.

Can so.

Not like my dad.

My dad plays the bagpipes.

They hurt my ears, I say.

It's music, explains George, his voice singsongy.

My dad says it sounds like a cat in heat.

What's a heated cat sound like?

A great answer jumps into my head. Mee-ouch, I say. Mee-ouch.

He should laugh. Are cats and dogs also God's children? he asks instead.

Sure.

Just like us?

Maybe less important, I answer. They have fur instead of skin. And they can't talk.

George nods. We're grown-up now, he says. Know how I know that?

I ask.

Because my mom told me.

George's mom has an English accent. She smells like lemons. I love her. At their house this morning, she said: Go on now, boys, and don't dawdle. *Dah-dol* is how the word sounded. First we looked for the Box Man at the Bumpity. Box Man, we shouted, kind of hoping we wouldn't find him: Come out and be a poo-poo butt! That was funny. Next we walked along Dunforest Avenue—Mister Dun's forest, Dad always says, except there is no forest and no Mister Dun—to Estelle. At the corner of Byng Avenue was a pile of garbage outside a house. In the pile was a highchair stained with stuff. Dead baby, said George. I didn't answer but inside I got chillied. I chased squirrels until I felt warm again. He kicked leaves.

Don't *dah-dol*, I told him.

We're early, he replied.

Our school is near Finch Avenue Public but also far away. You trot down a hill, keeping clear of cars and buses and the slippy slope into the ravine—no children get out of the ravine alive—and then you cross a street and climb another hill. Usually the streets and sidewalks are busy. George and me are early this morning, though. Real early. We're the first children ever to visit the planet earth. We're the last boys left in the universe.

I get chillied again.

Blessed Trinity School is also still closed. BTS on my sweater crest. Father, Son and the Holy Goat. The yard is huge. It goes on forever, until the other end. The sky is even huger. It goes on forever and ever. (Amen?) The sky goes on until it meets God.

What's behind the clouds? I ask George.

The sky.

What's behind the sky?

The sun.

What's behind the sun?

Heaven, I guess.

What's behind heaven?

He has to think about this one. His face scrunches. God? he asks.

Amen, I answer.

BTS goes on forever, until it ends. The doors are shut. The windows are mirrors. No kids or teachers. Just George and me, alone. Lonely boys, lonely and—

But then I notice stuff: cars in the parking lot and bikes locked to fences. Open drapes. Lights switched on.

Maybe we should try the door, I say.

We're early, he replies, not sure anymore.

The door isn't locked. The hallway is bright. Our class—morning kindergarten, Miss Malone—is through another set of doors. Grade One, Missus Nolan, is next to it. Voices come from that room. No way. I see children sitting at desks in the kindergarten. No way.

Boys!

Sister Mary Wyatt. Rounding the corner from the office, the ruler in her hand. She's the school principal. She's a penguin.

George tries to whistle. I start to cry.

They called our houses. They called the police. Everyone was looking for us. Everyone was worried. To death, even. Everyone was worried to death.

Do people die? I ask Mom at lunch.

Yes.

Will you die?

Some day.

And come back alive?

She smiles.

Will Dad die also?

Yes.

And you'll both come back alive to be with me and Toad and Puss again?

She rubs my forehead with her finger. What ideas you get, she says.

Will I die?

Not for a long, long time, she answers. For such a long time, you can't imagine it.

Yes I can.

She asks.

Imagine dying for a long time, I reply. For a billion million years. For a week.

Eat your lunch, says Mom.

I do, because I love her. I love you, Mom, I say.

I love you too.

The soup is chicken with rice, sipping once, sipping twice, and the sandwich is jam. A glass of milk. Two cookies. Best of all, no Toad. He's asleep, the way a baby should be.

Will Sister Mary Wyatt die? I ask.

Eventually.

Could she maybe die soon?

That's not nice.

She can come back later on, I say, my cheeks warm. When I'm finished at BTS.

You just want her to go away, says Mom.

Go away and die for a million hundred years, I answer. Then come back later on.

Sister Mary Wyatt should go away and come back later on. She carries a ruler and makes kids so scared they pee their pants and wipe snot onto their sleeves and say bad words in the washroom. She's the principal. She's a penguin.

I'm going to live for so long I can't imagine it. Longer than the schoolyard: taller than the sky. Behind the sky is the sun and behind the sun is heaven and behind heaven is God. God is my father. My dad is in construction. CON STRUCK SHUN. It doesn't hurt, though. I asked him.

Sliding down the stairs on my bum bum bum.

Don't hurt yourself, says Mom.

Okay, I answer. Only I sound like this: *ohohoh-kkk-eheheh*. Because I'm pushing off the top and sliding down the carpeted steps, slow then medium then fast, and then, *pow*, I'm on the mat at the bottom. Softest when boots cover the mat. Ouchiest when the floor is bare.

As a bum bum bum.

Be careful, says Mom.

Will I see Grandma at Christmas? I ask her later. She's tired, I can tell. Could do with a cup of tea. A few minutes alone on the couch.

I think so.

I'll be a good boy with her.

I know you will, answers Mom. She smiles, even though Toad is pinching her nose.

What does Grandma look like?

You remember.

Kind of.

She's your grandma.

Does she have white hair?

Orange and grey and white.

Spots on her hands?

You'll be seeing her soon, Charlie. You'll remember her then.

Of course I will! I think to myself. Can you play with me? I ask.

I have to change Toad. And fold laundry. And make the dinner.

I look at her again. She could do with a cup of tea. A few minutes alone on the couch. When I was little, I'd probably have cried and told her she didn't love me.

I'm a good boy, I say at the top of the stairs.

The best, answers Mom.

My grandma is called Grandma Ruthie. She's beautiful. (I just know it.) She had my dad. She comes to see us at Christmas and brings oozing chocolates and perfume kisses. She stays overnight and takes medicine. In the morning her room smells sweet. My grandpa lives on a farm. He has a moustache and bushy brows and silver hair. He smells smoky. A woman named Shirley gives us cookies and milk. She's the Wicked Witch.

My other grandma, who had my mom, doesn't have a name. My other grandpa doesn't have a name either. They spoke French. They live with God.

The light coming in my window is soft and warm and I'm sitting in it. In my room: on top of my bed. The light is from the sun and the sun is in heaven and heaven is where God—and my mom's mom and dad—lives. If I move, the light becomes a beam that leaves a shape on the floor. But I don't move. I want to be inside the light, inside the sun.

On Sunday we eat a bird. I'll carve, Moo, says Dad. Mom is Moo and my sister is Puss and the baby is Toad. I'm Sam Winkie. We used to live in Disneyland. With Mickey Mouse and Donald Duck and P-P-P-Porky Pig. Everyone there has special names. Dad called me Sam, for Yosemite Sam. I wore a cowboy hat and a red vest and I carried a gun in a belt. Mom called me Winkie, for Wee Willie Winkie. Once upon a time, while we were shopping in an apartment store, my parents got lost. In a deep forest. In a dark wood. They were lost, my mom and dad, and I was just a lonely boy, lonely and blue. So I decided to walk home to Disneyland. Mickey would send out a search party. Donald would call in the cavalry. I started on my way. Out the door, past the cars. I was all alone, all right, but I was also Wee Willie Winkie, running through the town. Upstairs and downstairs in his—

A man in a nightgown—a uniform, I guess—stopped me near a noisy road. He lifted me onto the counter in the store. They asked my name. I pulled out my gun and said: Stick 'em up, friend, or I'll blow you to kingdom come!

A woman made an announcement. *Would the parents of a boy named Sam Winkie please come to the service counter.*

Mom and Dad love telling that story to guests. He was walking up the ramp onto a six-lane highway! Dad loves to say. They laugh and laugh, though Mom always stops first. I don't laugh at all. They were lost in the woods, my mom and dad. I could have wound up a dorphin.

I'll cut the bird, Moo, repeats Dad.

The bird is dead. We're going to eat him. He's a turkey. Kids in Grade One call each other turkeys. Also goofs and sucks and spazzes and fatsoes. Mom kisses Toad on the belly and says she's going to eat him up. He pees. All the time, the boy pees.

Does that turkey have pee and poo inside him? I ask.

Charlie . . .

Gross, says Puss.

Poo poo, says Toad, who can't really talk.

It must be weird having thoughts in your head but not knowing how to say them. Even though you think, *I'd like some ham for lunch, please,* all you can say is, *Gaba hum, pheez.*

Who understands that? You might as well be a cat. A cat thinks, *Some tuna fish would be delish.* But a cat says, *Meeooww*, which is pretty useless. Even worse is a dog. Dogs are dying to talk to humans. *Let me lick your face*, they want to say. *I love you, yes I do yes I do YES I DO!* What are they stuck with? A bark or a thumping tail or a lick that makes you mad. Poor dog. Poor cat. Poor Toad. Words are the only way to let people know what you think. Words make all the difference.

The floor is an ocean and it's cool and fishy deep. The floor is an ocean and is full of sharks, peeps and crocodiles. Also monsters. Also fish sticks. Fall in and you're dead. Fall in and you're ketchup. Me, George and Pete are crowded on the couch. Careful, I warn them. A wind will blow you into the water. A wave will knock you into the sea. Pete is careful but George tries for the chair. Watch out, says Pete. George lands half on, half off.

Sharks! I shout.

Snaggleteeth nip at his ankles. Slimy tendrils rope him in. Pull him under. Into the black.

Made it, he says.

Your foot touched the rug, says Pete.

Did not.

Did so.

The shark ate my foot off, admits George.

Does it hurt?

It's chewed up and yucky, he says. Blood is gushing all over.

Pete and I look at his foot. I think of ketchup. Pete thinks of steak.

Your foot looks like steak, he says.

What's steak? asks George.

Bloody meat. My dad eats it.

My dad eats blood, too, I say. Stuck in a sausage. The smell is so stinky we have to leave the house. Or else we'll barf.

Gross, say the other boys.

We are quiet for a while. Pete and I dangle our legs over the couch. George bounces on the chair.

You can't breathe under water, I tell Pete.

You drown.

Drown dead.

Double dead, he says.

I push him off. He's surprised—I'm surprised I did it—and lands on his bum. Even more surprising, he starts to cry. Pete's ears stick out and his hair is prickly. He has a goofy grin. He's my best friend. One day, I held his penis while he peed on the Macgreevys' garden. He held mine, only I giggled and peed on his shoe. We got a glass from the kitchen to taste it. He dared me. I dared him back. Mom found us, though, and she was angry. Anyway, pee tastes awful. I've tried it. Almost.

You're a fish stick, I tell him.

He jumps up to pinch my nipples, the way we used to do. I punch him to make him stop. Mom comes into the room and I say, Sorry, Pete. He says sorry back.

Outside, orders Mom.

On the front steps George says: Gentlemen, you're probably wondering why I've called you here today.

It's cold out. Ants and bugs and worms are mostly already dead.

Toad is still a baby, I complain.

He's almost two.

He'll cry all night.

He's a good sleeper.

And he'll wet the bed.

She gives me a look. I get hot in the face.

But it's *my* room, I say.

It still will be.

Only half now.

Don't think that way. He's your brother.

Sorry.

He loves you.

And I . . . I mean, you know . . .

Yes I do, says Mom, kissing me on the forehead.

Never reveal the secret code, says Allan. He's a boy on our street who no one knows. His house, next to the Bumpity, is haunted. His parents are ghosts.

Gentlemen, I say, you're probably wondering why I've called you here today.

Leo-the-lion, Sylvester-the-cat, Snaggletooth Billie, Le Frog, Hair Rabbit, Puss-n-Boots, plus Bear One and Bear Two, at attention, sir! I position the cuddlies around me. Leo and Sylvester, my top guys, get the pillow: Le Frog and Hair Rabbit guard the wall. Billie rides shotgun. Boots keeps an eye on the window. Less important cuddlies live down at my feet. If they fall off, I won't be too sad. If monsters eat them, my heart won't be broken.

Poor Sylvester, I say to the cat, now a scarface. You'll never be the same again.

I'm okay, he answers.

Will you still protect me?

We all will, replies Leo.

That makes me feel great. Love you guys, I say, giving them kisses.

Poo-poo butt, calls a tiny voice from the other side of the room.

Quiet, I say to him. You're a baby. You're supposed to be asleep.

He shouts for his mom.

It's *my* room, I tell the opening door.

I turn into a lamb. No, I ask a magic lamb to take me on a ride. He promises it will be safe. He promises to look after me. We fly up into the sky and stop on a cloud. Let's keep going to heaven, I say. Too far, answers the lamb. Kids can't fly that high.

Dad is watching TV. His coffee is steaming in a cup. His pipe is smoking in a dish. While he watches, he carves pieces of wood and glues them into model ships. Wood chips fly onto the floor and into his coffee. Some of them end up in his hair.

Can I be the first boy to visit the centre of the earth? I ask him.

What?

I say it again.

What do you think, Moo? he says. Can Yosemite Sam be the first boy to visit the centre of the earth?

Sure, she replies.

Okay, he tells me.

Great! I say. Then: Dad?

Mmm?

Want me to brush the wood from your hair?

Look up, I say to George on the way home from school one day. Look waaay up.

Do you think the Friendly Giant is real?

Sure.

Rusty the Rooster and Jerome the Giraffe?

Double sure.

But Captain Kangeroo isn't a kangeroo?

That's different, I answer, not certain why.

We walk another block.

Do you believe that Jack climbed a beanstalk and found a giant up there? I ask.

Sure.

And do you believe Jack stepped onto a cloud?

Maybe he met the Friendly Giant, answers George.

Look up, I say. Look waaay up.

How was school today? Mom asks me.

We're trying to drink tea at the kitchen table. Mom said Toad could bang pots for a few minutes. Turns out he bangs them loud and sings *lalalalalala.* Her tea is real: mine is water. I take two cookies from the plate.

Billy Neary got sent behind the piano, I answer. He spit paper at some girls.

Did he?

Lenny Grusa sat back there all day yesterday.

Again?

He's a hard boy.

What else happened?

Something. Something that made me feel cold and lonely and wanting to be home in my room.

Nothing, I reply.

She rubs my forehead again. Those lines, she says. They tell me different.

Miss Malone is beautiful.

Of course she is.

I love her.

I know.

I love you and Dad, too. And Puss. And Josy-the-cat.

What about Toad?

Can I have two more cookies?

How many have you eaten?

And Toad, I add. I love him tons.

Take two, says Mom.

Four chocolate chip cookies! The most, so far.

He says it again the next day. Miss Malone has just handed us crayons and paper when this boy, Jimmy Reilly, leans across the desk and drops the same words into my ear.

Miss Malone has snakes in her legs, he whispers.

I get chillied.

Can't you see them?

Miss Malone wheezes when she walks and spits when she shouts. Her dress hangs to her knees. Her legs are puffy. Running up and down her skin are lines the colour of bruises. The lines are too dark to be crayon. Also, when she walks, they sort of bulge, as if they're—

They move, says Jimmy.

No they don't.

Watch.

I don't want to.

Like snakes in the grass, he adds. We have them at our cottage.

Though I stare at him, I actually want to cry. You have freckles all over your face, I say.

So do you.

What?

Not so much talking, says Miss Malone. Everyone draw their favourite animal.

I draw Josy. I try not to look at Jimmy Reilly's paper. He draws squiggly, snaky lines, then looks up at me and smiles. I hate him. I love Miss Malone. I don't have freckles all over my face: he does.

The ravine is out of bounds. Good boys and girls don't go down there. Thorn bushes cover the slope. Shopping carts fill the stream. Once, a long time ago, a Grade Two kid saw a fridge floating in the water. He found a frozen boy in it. Even more dangerous is the hole the stream pours into. Children have gone into the hole, but none have come out. An older kid told Lenny Grusa that the hole is a magic wardrobe. (He meant a closet.) Close the door and another one opens. Then another and another, until you reach the centre of the earth.

George and I are walking up Finch Avenue above the ravine. I keep to the outside. Sometimes I end up with one foot on the sidewalk, one foot on the road. That gives me a limp.

Grade Fours smoke cigarettes down there, says the boy Jimmy. He's out of breath from running. His words are clouds. His cheeks are pink.

Yeah? says George.

They hide in the culvert so teachers won't find them.

How do you know? I ask, feeling tingly.

I watch.

In the ravine?

He nods.

You're not allowed, I tell him. I want to say more—maybe about his freckles, for sure about his jacket, which is buttoned wrong—but I don't.

They also kiss each other, he adds.

Who does?

Big kids. Grade Fours and Fives. Girls with boys. Smack on the lips.

Smack is a great word. Like a bum on a toilet seat.

Yuck, says George.

We keep walking.

What do you think happens if you stand on a cloud? I ask Jimmy.

God tells you to be careful.

Do you fall through?

No way, he answers. You bounce up and down.

And you don't fall?

Never.

I turn to George. Told you, I say.

Okay, he replies.

Jimmy stops and looks at my leg. Why are you limping? he asks.

I'm not.

Yes you—

Your coat is done up wrong, I say. There's an extra button at the bottom.

George and I have to cross Finch Avenue at the crosswalk and turn onto Estelle.

Where do you live? I ask Jimmy.

In Ireland.

Is that near? asks George.

Just up there, he answers, pointing.

He runs ahead. Miss Malone has snakes in her legs! he shouts back at us.

Where's Ireland? I ask Mom. She puts my lunch—a peanut butter sandwich and chips—on the table. Toad is already eating, if you can call it that. Most of a sandwich and an entire banana are squish. Some of the squish is sliming up his nose; some of it is oozing off his chin.

In Europe.

Near the soupy Nile?

She smiles. I'll read to you later on, she says. Then: Toad, be careful with your—

The lid is off his cup. Milk pours onto the floor.

Is Ireland a hundred miles away?

Mom squeezes a cloth in the sink.

A million hundred miles?

Huh? she replies. It's across the— Don't play in it! she shouts at him.

Toad has milk spots on his face.

Can I go there?

She mops up.

After lunch, I repeat. Can I go to—

Fine, fine.

Now he slaps the highchair with his hands. Mom gets a milk and squish shower.

Toad! she says again.

Muck, he answers. He probably means *milk*, but he can't really talk.

I run into Pete outside.

I'm going to Ireland, I say. Want to come?

We head up the road towards the Bumpity. Pete doesn't walk to school, like George and me: his mom drives him. Except for the route to BTS, I haven't done much walking either. I only know Dunview Avenue; I only know our block. That's enough, says Dad. That's the neighbourhood, says Mom. At one end of the block is a field for picking flowers and blueberries. At the other end is the Bumpity. It's also a field, with trees and bushes and a path. The path is bumpy on a bike, so kids call the place the Bumpity. Dad says houses will be built at both ends. He says it's bound to happen. No one lives there now, though. Only skunks and raccoons and stray cats. Only the Box Man.

You ever seen the Box Man? I ask Pete.

Sure.

What did he look like?

He was in a box.

Even though it's close by, the Bumpity feels far away. Feels exciting and scary: feels great, most days. Tall trees shake. Leaves float down. Birds caw caw or chirp chirp. Dead animals turn smelly. And the Box Man: he's always there, no one knows why, no one knows where.

We're here, I say at the corner.

Where?

Ireland.

Pete frowns.

Across a wide ocean and a chicken sea, I explain. IN YOUR UP. Full of men wearing hoods and snaggletooth dragons and monsters oozing slime.

Let's fight them.

We need sticks.

We attack the bushes with sticks. Come out, monsters, we shout. You can't run but you can hide!

He stops. What about the Box Man? Suppose we accidentally hit him with a stick?

He doesn't live in Ireland.

You sure?

Positive.

Yahoo! says Pete, and whacks a bush. His ears stick out and he has a goofy grin. He and I used to hold each other's penises. He's my best friend.

Never reveal the secret code, says Allan. His house is right beside the Bumpity. Paint peels off the walls; curtains are always closed. No one cuts the grass. No one cleans up the yard. Cats sit on every porch on the block, except his. Birds never land on that roof.

Okay, we answer, and run.

When is Christmas, Mom?

She doesn't answer. Toad's diaper is stinking and the

sink is full of dishes. No doubt about it: she could do with a cup of tea. A few minutes alone on the couch.

I ask again.

In a million years, she replies.

I think it's in six weeks.

She smiles.

Isn't Christmas in six weeks?

I was just kidding.

Six weeks *and* a million years, I say.

Toad screams until she picks him up. Right away, he starts kicking to be put back down.

Out of the kitchen, you two, she says.

Me?

Come on, says Mom, pushing us through the doorway. I just need fifteen minutes to—

You *never* talk to me! I say.

She sends us down to the playroom. Poor Mom. The baby is a lot of work right now.

Toad should be asleep.

You asleep, Toad?

Nothing.

Toad, I repeat. You better be asleep. Okay?

The room is dark. The dark is black. Mom, Dad and Puss are all gone away. Drowned in the hole in the basement. Drowned and flown up to heaven.

Don't cry, Leo, I tell my lion. There there, I say to Sylvester-the-cat.

Poor cuddlies.

I sing to them: *I'm just a lonely boy / Lonely and blue / I'm all alone / with nothing to do.*

Who can blame them? Monsters under the bed so you can't get up. Monsters in the closet so you won't reach the door alive.

Toad!

He should know. He should know that if a monster attacks his crib first—babies *do* taste sweeter—I won't be able to help him. Step on the floor and a monster arm will grab my foot. Drag me under. Eat me up.

Babies taste sweeter than small boys, I tell the darkness.

The cuddlies are sobbing again. Love you guys, I say, squeezing Leo and Sylvester and Billie and Le Frog. Love you all.

We know. Thanks.

Toad!!

A sound. He's crying.

Quiet, I whisper.

More sounds. From beyond the door. From outside the room. Someone is coming. Someone is—

Everything all right? she asks in a sleepy voice.

Toad woke me up, I answer.

Now he's really bawling. What a baby. A sucky baby boy.

Shh, says Mom. Go back to sleep.

Shh, I say to my cuddlies. Go back to sleep.

She takes ages to finish with him. I wait, watching her in the dark. Finally, she crosses the room and sits on the bed. I feel sleepy already.

I tried singing Toad back to sleep, I say.

What did you sing, Charlie?

The song.

She tucks me in. Her lips are cold. Her hands are cold too. The air is black but I can still see her eyes.

Would you sing it for me now?

Like when I was a baby?

In the rocking chair upstairs, she answers. You'd promise not to cry. Don't worry, Mommy, you'd say. I won't cry this time.

But I would?

Your chin would quiver. Your eyes would fill with tears.

Every time?

Without fail.

That makes me dreamy, closer to sleep. I was just a kid then, I say.

Now you're all grown-up.

I sing the song so only Mom can hear it. Only her and me. No way I'll cry about the lonely boy. Lonely and blue. He's all alone, with nothing—

She wipes my cheeks with a tissue.

Lagra newlie, I hum once she's gone, *danler tomp / Soater soater / touler tomp!* Are these words? The words to another song? I always think of them when Mom is with me. They make me think of her.

I know what a monster looks like, says George.

What?

Slime.

What's slime look like? I ask.

Goo.

Pus, answers Pete.

Yeah, I say.

You can't see ghosts, you know, says George.

They're visible, adds Pete.

You can't see monsters either, I say.

Except in the dark, replies Pete.

Then they're all black, says George.

And slimy.

Pus, I say, because the word feels great on my tongue. Witches, goblins and ghosts are all slimy and black and oozy with pus.

Yeah, say the other boys.

Dear Santa,

My mom is writing this because I can't make words yet. Only drawings and circles and XXXs and OOOs. I've been a good boy all year. The bad things I did were kid stuff. Nothing terrible, except the time George and I were late for school. Miss Malone didn't even send us behind the piano. I've never been behind the piano. Billy has. Lenny Grusa gets put there almost every day. Please send me:

1. a GI Joe

2. two Dinky cars (not red)

3. Silly Putty

Mom says I can only ask for three things. I know you can leave more gifts, if you want to. It's your decision. I'm just a small good boy.

Love,

Charlie Foran

P.S. No more Lego, please.

Men are in space. It's true. Not like boats on the sea: like fish inside the sea. Floating men, called ASTRO NAUTS, count stars from the window. Eat slices of moon cheese. Drink the Milky Way. Space is above the sky but below heaven. The moon is in space. So are the sun and the stars. It must be crowded. Lonely too. Because you can't leave your ship to visit other ASTRO NAUTS. You can't play outside. There isn't any air in space. On earth, there's loads. Plenty for animals and plants and fishes, even though they breathe water. (I've tried it: no good.) Air is everywhere down here. We just can't see it. Up there, space is everywhere as well. We just can't breathe it.

Space is the place between us and God.

Mom is reading the newspaper while I eat cookies and drink milk. Hey, I say to her, noticing a photograph. That's like the thing in Parkview Park. She looks at me.

You mean you don't know what that is? she asks. I'm only five, I answer. Of course, she says. Well, now you do. On Saturday Dad drives me to Parkview—it's too far to walk alone—and I race to the thing like the thing in the newspaper. Suddenly it looks amazing. Suddenly I'm scared. Climb up, says Dad. Blast off to the moon. D-a-a-d, I answer. I stand in front of the ladder for ages. Snowflakes bomb my eyes. The wind puffs my jacket. Just when he's about to get mad, I grab the bar. One, two, three steps and I'm up. Inside. Inside the body. The floor is rows of metal with slits in between; bars make up the walls. I kneel for a while, my knees sore, then lie on my stomach. No way I'll go higher. No way I'll climb into the ball at the top.

We'll come back on a warmer day, says Dad.

Suppose it's up in space by then?

The ship will wait for you.

Promise?

Promise, he answers.

Blow into the tissue, says Mom.

I am.

Harder.

I blow harder. The snot still won't come out.

You're using your mouth, she says. Try blowing from your nose.

How do I do that?

Press your lips together. Force the air—

I try again. My cheeks puff. Mom! I say.

You'll learn.

It's stupid.

You'll learn soon enough.

Jimmy wants to play Joseph in the Christmas pageant. He asks Miss Malone if he can. She says, Sorry, too late. She's already told John Sealy he can play Joseph. Then Jimmy asks about the three wise guys. Miss Malone smiles and calls him bold. It turns out the Three Wise Men are taken as well. She hopes he isn't disappointed.

They aren't just wise guys, he tells me. They're kings from faraway lands.

Ireland? I ask.

What?

Are the kings from Ireland?

I think so.

I'm a shepherd, I say.

So am I.

Miss Malone says we have to wear towels on our heads.

Some of the other boys play animals, says Jimmy. That's way worse.

I'd hate to be a mooo cow.

Or a baaa goat, he adds.

We giggle.

Quiet, boys, says Miss Malone. If you can't sit nicely like the rest of the children, I'll have no choice but to put you at separate desks.

Or behind the piano, whispers Jimmy.

Shh, I answer.

For so long, she forgets we're back there and we turn into mummies.

I lower my eyes to make him stop.

Time to rehearse our pageant, says Miss Malone. She stands behind Jimmy's chair and rests her hands on his shoulders. Another word, and it's the piano for him. I figure it's okay to look at her hands. Her fingers are stubby and her skin is stained. Her nails aren't lollipops. I promised myself I wouldn't look farther down, but I do. I can't help looking below her dress and I can't help seeing.

Miss Malone is still beautiful. I'll always love her.

She has snakes in her legs.

Here's what happened to Sylvester-the-cat. Once upon a time we were driving on the highway to Blind River. Sylvester told me he wasn't feeling well. He said he was going to barf. I knew it would be gross—Toad did it all the time—so I stuck him out the window. Leo-the-lion warned me that the wind loved to snatch children and blow them into the sky. Puss, who was colouring a picture on the window sill, said: Don't fall out yourself, ha ha. But then the wind *did* grab Sylvester. It bit my hand until I let him go.

I cried.

Stop the car, Dave, said Mom.

Dad pulled over.

Bet he's all smushed, said Puss.

Shut up, I told her.

Cars whooshed past us on the highway. The ground grumbled under our feet. A raccoon *was* smushed on the pavement. Flies swam in its ketchup blood. Its eyes were gone. Dad squeezed my hand. His skin was rough and warm and I decided that I missed being carried on his shoulders. I loved rubbing his hair and scratching his chin and covering his eyes until he said: Look out! I loved his smell.

Sylvester lay on the white line, legs crossed, head twisted sideways. He looked relaxed. He looked okay. I was ready to rush onto the highway when Dad stopped me. A truck piled with logs got bigger and louder and started firing dust and stones at us. Dad made a circle around my neck with his fingers. I blocked my face.

When I pulled my hands away, Sylvester-the-cat was doing somersaults. One, two, three.

Ouch, said Dad.

We rescued him. Both hims—he was in pieces. First, I was amazed: a split kitty. Then I guess I cried again.

Dad hoisted me onto his shoulders. *Aaaagh*, he said, because I was getting too big for this. Back at the car, I showed the cuddlie to Mom.

I think I can fix him, she said.

Tire mark, said Dad, pointing.

Looks like a raccoon, said Puss. She picked at the stuffing coming out his leg. Hope he doesn't start to stink.

Shut up, I told her again.

Mom scolded me this time.

Dad calls him Scarface now. You dirty rat, he says. You killed my brother. I keep telling him Sylvester is a cat. And he's clean, I say. Mom put him in the washing machine, twice.

Pete goes to a different school from George and me. He's not Catholic. He's something else. Lots of people aren't Catholic, says Mom. Our church, also called Blessed Trinity, isn't even there yet. It's CON STRUCK SHUN. Sister Mary Wyatt walked our class across Bayview Avenue to a field of holes and dirt piles and men wearing turtle shells. She stopped near some bricks. Look here, children, she said. This is where God's house will be. Where's God now? asked Billy Neary. Sister Mary answered his question, but I didn't hear it. Jimmy Reilly was whispering in my ear. He's staying in a motel, he said. With TV and an outdoor pool.

Does your school have a principal? I ask Pete on the front steps of my house.

Mister Macdonald, he answers.

Is he a penguin?

I don't think so.

Do you go to church on Sundays?

Yup.

Is it built?

He doesn't understand the question.

Our church isn't even built, I explain. It's just bricks and dirt and stuff.

Must be cold to sit in, he says.

Cold on my bum.

Your big fat bum?

We giggle. Then we think a bit.

Do you have to keep quiet in church? I ask.

Shhhhhhhhhhhhhhhhhhhhhhhhhh, answers Pete, until all the breath is out of his mouth. I get a chocolate bar if I'm a good boy.

You're not a good boy.

Yes I am.

No you're not.

Pete tackles me in the ditch. We'll get wet! I shout. Tough, he answers, pinning my arms. Bad enough that he still wants to pinch nipples. Worse is that he won't stop, even if I say uncle.

I'm wearing a sweater and jacket, so it doesn't hurt. But my pants get soaked and my hair grows icicles. This is dumb, I tell him.

It's fun, he answers.

Dumb, I repeat.

Pete's face scrunches up. Before any tears show, he races across the street. The bum of his pants is a stain, as if he peed himself.

Never reveal the secret code, says Allan.

(What kind of a boy is Allan? asked Mom as we walked past his house one day. A ghost boy, I answered. Trapped inside a ghost house. He eats worms and drinks blood and howls at the moon. His only friends are giants with bad breath. Is that true? she said. Pete told me, I replied. And George. They told me everything I know about Allan.)

Dad is hammering nails into wood. The hammer goes *tick tock* and the nail says *ouch ouch* until it gets swallowed by the board. He is building a fence between our house and the Macgreevys'. To make the backyard safe for Toad to play in, he explains. Safe for Toad and fine by me. Missus Macgreevy is a witch: Mister Macgreevy is an ogre.

Can I be the first boy in history to fly up to the moon? I ask my dad.

In history?

Since forever.

He stands up. It must be hard to do, because he groans. How will you get there, he asks. The rocket ship?

Wings, I answer.

You have wings under your jacket?

Under my skin, I say. I have to speak the magic words to make them appear.

Puss is supposed to be raking leaves to earn her allowance. Instead, she's blowing clouds from her mouth and playing hopscotch on the patio.

Can Sam Winkie be the first boy to fly to the moon? Dad asks her.

Dad . . . , I say.

He's making stuff up again, answers Puss.

He told me he has wings under his skin.

That's just because he wasn't picked to be an angel in the Christmas pageant.

My cheeks get warm.

Of course you can be the first boy, says Dad quickly. He ruffles my hair. The first boy in history.

Puss makes a face at me.

Of course you can be, son, he repeats, kneeling back down. You and no one else.

I make a face at her.

Ouch ouch, cries another nail.

Wonderful, Miss Malone tells us outside the school gym. You all look wonderful.

She isn't wearing her flower dress this afternoon; she's in a special gown. The gown is black with silver stuff stuck to the collar. The shoes on her feet are shiny enough to tap tap together. Her cheeks are pink—for the holiday season—and her lips are candy canes. Miss Malone is more Christmassy than Sister Mary Wyatt. The principal can't help being a penguin, I guess. She can't help being black and white.

Lovely, says Sister Mary. And where are my beautiful angels?

The angels step forward.

You look heavenly, girls, she says.

Girls? I look at the angels: all of them—all six—are girls.

The principal runs her hands through Brenda Deane's wings. I've felt the wings and know how soft they are: softer than Leo's fur, softer than Toad's bum. (Mom says that: I think his bum is disgusting.) Still, Sister Mary Wyatt shouldn't smile and sigh and touch first Brenda's cheek, then the cheeks of the other angel girls. She should at least say hello to the shepherds. She should—

Here are Joseph and Mary and the Three Wise Men, says Miss Malone. And these boys are the shepherds.

I keep my head down.

Beautiful angels, says the principal, not even looking at Jimmy and me.

I asked Mom to read aloud about penguins once. Penguins eat fish without cooking them. Skin and scales, bones and tails; they wolf down entire fishes, sometimes while the poor things are still squirming. Even though they're supposed to be birds, penguins can't fly. They can only wobble on rocks and swim in ice cubes. Instead of nice singing, they make stupid squawking noises. Squawk, squawk, squawk. Stupid, stupid, stupid.

I've been watching my flock for ages. In my bathrobe. With a towel wrapped around my head. Mary and Joseph have already walked up from the back while Grade One kids sang a song about the little town of Bethlehem, and Joanne Kuri, God's arch angel, has already flown up to us poor shepherds and said: Unto you a child is born. Now Jimmy is pointing with his staff, a tree branch his dad cut in a forest. (Mine is a hockey stick.) Look, says Jimmy to me and Lucci Pavese, a bright star in the night sky.

I look. Lucci is too busy trying to keep his beard on his

face. Only the wise guys are allowed to have beards. But his dad made him one and now *he's* a real shepherd, while me and Jimmy are goofs in bathrobes and towels.

It's a sign, I reply. Seeing Mom in the audience, I smile. (Don't wave, she told me this morning. A smile will be fine.)

Yes, says Jimmy.

Lucci Pavese is supposed to talk now. We're supposed to listen to him and then walk to the front, where a bunch of kids dressed as cows and sheep, and John Sealy in a car blanket on one knee, and Margaret Mahoney, who's Mary Virgin, lying in some hay with a scarf on her head, are pretending to be in a stable. (No room in the motel.) The three wise guys come next, singing a song about Orient kings. Then the angels, flapping their wings and singing at the end. Singing for Sister Mary Wyatt. Sister Mary, with a fishtail in her mouth.

It's a sign, I repeat.

Lucci's beard is dangling from his cheek the way spaghetti does when Toad eats it. Grown-ups are laughing. He's ready to bawl.

Go to Bethlehem, shepherds, whispers the voice of Miss Malone. Right away.

We reach the stable.

Kind shepherds, says John. Welcome.

Hi, we say.

More giggles.

What child is this? says one of the wise guys. His name is Gregory Simic and his beard is green. Miss Malone told him that kings don't have green beards. Gregory said they do in Ireland.

Come, says Lucci suddenly, holding his beard up with his hand. Let us go to Beth-ham.

We're already there, answers Jimmy.

Some angels decide to sing: *Away in a manger / No crib for a—*

Not yet, girls, says the voice of Sister Mary. Let Mary and Joseph finish.

Behold the son of God, announces John. He's been practising the word *behold* in class. Behold my pencil, he'd say. Also, Behold my nose. One day Lenny Grusa said, Behold my weenie, and Miss Malone sent him behind the piano.

Behold, says John again. The baby is over his head.

I want to watch him behold the baby, but my towel keeps coming undone. I'm fixing it when my staff kind of swings loose. It kind of knocks Joseph on the arm and Joseph kind of drops Jesus. The baby bounces on the floor.

My God, says the voice of Miss Malone.

Sing, angels! says Sister Mary.

No one sings. We all stare at baby Jesus. He's naked. His eyelashes are pretty. He has no penis.

Where's his—? asks Jimmy.

My baby! cries Mary Virgin.

It's just a doll, says a cow.

Bad shepherd, says John to me.

Pick her up, says Jimmy to Joseph. And *you're* a bad Joseph.

John picks up the doll and raises it back over his head.

Behold—

The son of God, say the wise guys.

They fall to their knees. The animals fall to their knees.

We shepherds fall last, except for the angels, who don't fall at all: they turn to the audience and spread their wings to fly home to heaven.

Sing, angels, repeats Sister Mary. Please!

Angels and Grade One kids sing: *Away in a manger / No crib for a bed / The little Lord Jesus / Lay down his sweet head.*

We all join in for the next one (my favourite): *The first Noel / The angel did say / Was to certain poor shepherds / In fields as they lay.*

Miss Malone claps the loudest. Wonderful, she tells us as we walk down the aisle.

Sorry, I say to her.

In the hallway, moms and grandparents give their children and grandchildren kisses. I see only one dad and he stands by himself in a corner. Mom kisses me on both cheeks and says I did great, even though she knows and I know that I did a terrible thing.

Gregory Simic's grandfather shakes his hand. He is a tall man with white hair and sparkly brown eyes. Though he also speaks with an accent, it isn't the same as Missus Campbell's. I stare at him until Mom asks if I'm okay. Later, Santa Claus visits our classroom. His eyes are sparkly brown and his voice is so familiar I get confused, and don't answer his question. He just says, Ho ho ho, and gives me a gift. Miss Malone tells us we can open them right away. Mine is crayons and paper. Jimmy's is crayons and paper too. John Sealy, Lenny Grusa, Billy Neary, Lucci Pavese: all us boys get crayons and paper. Girls get pencils and a colouring book. The angels as well. Nothing special for them from Santa.

Dad is tucking me into bed.

I heard about the pageant, he says.

Jesus fell.

Guess he had no wings.

Only angels have wings, I say, and only girls get to be angels. It's not fair. It's also dangerous.

Dangerous?

To boys like baby Jesus, I explain. If he'd had wings, he wouldn't have, you know, bounced.

Jesus bounced?

Boingy, boingy, I say, using Leo to show how it happened.

Next time you'll be an angel, he replies.

No point in telling Dad, but there won't be a next time. For me or for other boys. Not in ten weeks. Not in five million hundred years. Grade One kids sing carols at the pageant. Grade Two children go to a special mass with their parents. After that, you grow up. After that, you die.

He says good night.

Can you read me *Chicken Soup* just once? I ask.

You have the book memorized, he answers. Turn the pages yourself.

It's too dark.

Not tonight, Charlie.

Then can you check?

He groans.

Please?

He groans again and sinks to one knee. His head disappears below the mattress. His voice sounds far away.

No monsters down here, he calls.

Did you feel with your hands?

The coast is clear, says Dad.

But they come back. The minute he leaves, they start to bump my mattress with their heads. Worse, he accidentally shut the door. Except for a yellow blur around the night light, the dark is black. I forgot to pee and now I need to. No way I'll make it alive, though. Not a chance.

Leo suggests I stick my penis in the water glass. I did that once: big mess. Sylvester says we need to be certain about the monsters. I've already been splatted by a truck, he tells us both. What could a monster do? I dangle him upside down over the side. When I feel the top of his head touch the floor, I slide him the length of the bed. He begs me to pull him back up. His hair is on end. His eyes are wild.

Loads of them, he says.

No!

Slimy and oozy and full of pus.

No!

Ready to grab your leg and drag you under and eat you up, like a fish stick.

Toad? I say loudly. Don't even think about getting up tonight, Toad.

Nothing.

I know you're not asleep. So I want to tell you to keep your feet off the floor. Not even a toe. Not even a toenail.

Silence.

Have they already eaten him? That makes me feel sweaty and excited. I gather up my cuddlies. Don't touch the wall, I warn them. Keep away from the end. Curl into a ball. Pretend you're asleep.

Not fair, not fair, not fair.

The bed is flying, like Dorothy's house before it crashed down and squashed a witch. Flying high into the sky. Stuff slips off and falls to the earth: blankets and pillows, less important stuffed animals. The bed stops on a cloud. The cloud is as fluffy as angel wings and as gentle as angel hair and is a place where humans can talk with friendly angel faces. Mom is on the cloud. She has pink wings and white hair. I say, Mom, if you're an angel, does that mean you're—

I awaken to the wet and to a smell. The wet, already cold, isn't just in the bum; it's also down my legs and across my back. The smell is sour.

It's okay, Charlie.

My pyjamas are being taken off and the sheets are being removed. My skin is wiped with a cloth. I'm told first to stand, put my arms through this and my legs through that, and then to lie back down. I'm told to blow my nose into a tissue and for once it works. Gunk shoots out and my cheeks don't balloon. Finally, I'm told to close my eyes. Everything is okay. Because they love me, love me very much.

Everything's okay, right, Mom? I say, thinking that she and I need to talk.

Don't worry about a thing.

I won't.

What do we need to talk about? I ask myself.

I'm sure ready to sleep now, she says. Ready to sleep through the night. Better go to bed.

It's nice in bed, I answer.

Safe and warm and cozy.

Mmm, I say. I look up at her eyes. In the dark, in the black. I see me in there. In the mirrors, I mean: the mirrors in her eyes.

You can go, I tell her.

More strange words—also a song, I think—come into my head once she's left. *Surlypon avyon*, I hum, *ony-dassy, ony-dassy*. Is the song about her? I bet it is.

At breakfast I remember what I wanted to talk to Mom about. What happened next? I ask her.

Next?

In the dream. We were in it together. You and me. What did we do after we left the cloud?

She stops buttering toast. I was in your dream? . . .

We were both there. You remember being on a cloud, don't you?

The knife is still in the air. Uh, sure, says Mom.

You have to remember, I say. You were right there inside it, with me.

Inside your room?

Inside my dream.

Puss says she'll be late for school. Toad calls for his BECKFEST. She brings the plate of toast to the table. What happened is this, she says slowly. We all lived happily ever after.

Oh Mom.

I was a good boy this year, I tell Jimmy. Santa is going to give me tons of presents.

Me too.

You weren't as good, I say, checking to make sure Miss Malone isn't watching us. Remember when you told me and George you snuck down into the ravine?

So?

That was naughty. You'll get less—

Boys!

We stiffen. I do, at least: Jimmy just grins. He's a funny kid. Not bad, like Lenny or Billy, but not good either, like John Sealy or Pat Sullivan or me, I guess.

Miss Malone is fit to be tied this morning. That's what she said once we were seated: I'm fit to be tied this morning, children. Brenda Deane told Joanne Kuri told the girl in the next desk that her mom called Sister Mary Wyatt after the pageant and asked, Was it really appropriate—A PRO PRE IT—for kindergarten children to be acting out the birth of Jesus Christ? I don't know what A PRO PRE IT means—I don't think anyone does—but I know that Miss Malone is fit to be tied. Other kids know it as well.

I lied, says Jimmy in a whisper.

Quiet, I should answer.

I never went down into the ravine, he adds, his eyes flying around his head. Some older boys did and I heard them talking about it. I'm going to get as many presents as you. I'm a good—

Charlie Foran and Jimmy Reilly!

My heart jumps into my throat.

If you two need to talk so badly, she says, why don't we find you a more private place, so you won't disrupt my class any longer.

Sorry, I try to say.

She says—

No!

She says—

Can't be.

Behind the piano, commands Miss Malone. Right now.

But— I say.

Enough out of you, young man. One apology for making trouble is more than I want to hear.

I could fall down. Fall down and go to sleep. Go to sleep and get smaller. Until I fit inside a rabbit hole. Until I fit into a crack in the earth.

Come on, says Jimmy.

My legs, I answer.

Don't pee your pants.

Lucky you boys are still in kindergarten, says Miss Malone, her voice mean. Otherwise, I'd march you down to Sister Mary's office this instant.

Snake lady, mumbles Jimmy.

The piano is next to the supply closet. I stole a peek behind it one day and got chillied: the space was skinny and dark, and you had to stand either facing the wall or the back of the piano. Jimmy and I barely fit. I'm not worried that I'll wet myself but I am worried that I'll sniffle. He makes a funny face and I feel better.

She isn't mad at us, he whispers.

No?

She never puts bad kids in with each other.

No talking, calls her voice.

Sorry, I call back.

A boy died in here once, says Jimmy.

Really?

Of starving and not drinking water. Miss Malone kept him behind the piano for so long his tongue fell out of his mouth and his eyes rolled around on the floor.

Bumps rise on my arms.

Do you believe me?

His eyes became marbles, I reply. One rolled up to the front of the class and stopped at her desk.

Jimmy sniggers.

The eyes looked at Miss Malone, I say, now feeling as if

I could float. Looked at her for ten hundred hours, until she started to cry.

And to apologize.

Don't put out my eyes. Apologize!

We snigger together. That word sounds as if you're actually doing it. Laughing through your nose. Snorting.

Quiet in there.

Jimmy stares at me. He doesn't need to: I won't call out, Sorry!

Your cheeks are pink, he says.

So are yours.

It's the freckles, he explains, touching his own face. They make you embarrassed. You have them, too, you know.

I know I do, I answer. I feel so light, so feathery light, I could drift up into the clouds. But not as many as you or my dad, I say.

Your dad has freckles?

And orange hair.

He thinks for a bit. My dad's right off the boat, he says. Is yours?

He drives a car.

Oh.

The class is singing a Christmas carol now, so we can talk as loud as we want.

Do you think Miss Malone will tell our parents? I ask.

I hope not, replies Jimmy. His smile goes away.

I'm sure she won't, I add to make him happy.

A shadow fills the back wall. Her face appears around the corner. Both of us jump.

Don't you boys want to come out? asks Miss Malone.

Yes, we say.

Then why didn't you answer when I called?

We're right off the boat, says Jimmy.

I'm disappointed in you, Charlie, says Miss Malone.

Don't say sorry to her, I tell myself. Sorry, Miss Malone, I reply.

Kids push past me to the door. Her desk is covered in presents and flowers. I stare at the gifts, not sure why.

What have you to say for yourself?

Nothing.

Nothing?

I didn't mean to knock John with my hockey stick, I finally answer.

About your behaviour with Mister Reilly, she says. I expected better. I *expect* better, from a boy like you.

Only when I'm in the corridor do I remember what is in my knapsack: a glass ball that I helped Mom choose at the drugstore and wrap up in the kitchen. I could return to the classroom and give Miss Malone her present. I could do that.

Why didn't you go back? asks Mom at the house. She has emptied my bag and found the gift.

I forgot.

Didn't you see other children leaving presents for Miss Malone?

No, I lie. Suddenly I think about Santa and about acting bad so soon before Christmas. I saw them, I say. But then I forgot. Nothing else happened at school today. Nothing bad. Honest.

Don't cry, she says, rubbing above my eyes with her finger and thumb.

Why does she keep doing that?

If those lines get any deeper, adds Mom, they'll never smooth out.

Toad is at it again: splashing soup and squishing bread in his highchair. He's also laughing and saying *skishy*. She gets a cloth.

I'll drop the gift off at school next week, she says with a sigh.

Tired? I ask her, the way Dad does. Only he kisses her in the middle of her forehead and says: Tired, Moo?

She smiles.

Does Toad have any freckles under that gunk? I ask.

She keeps smiling.

Skishy, repeats Toad, sliming some peanut butter between his fingers.

He's getting to be such a big boy, isn't he?

Sure, Mom, I answer.

Toad isn't a big boy at all. He can't talk. Saying *skishy* for squishy and *muck* for milk and *poo-poo butt* for just about everything else means you're still a baby. Take a peeled banana and a peanut butter sandwich and put them on a plastic plate. Give the plate to a kid. If he makes squish, he's still a baby. If he can *make up* a word like squish, he's a boy. Toad's mess. My word.

When's Christmas? I ask Mom that same day. She is filling the washing machine with clothes.

Monday.

Will Grandma Ruthie be here?

Dad is going to pick her up on Sunday afternoon.

Does she live far away?

Not far.

I thought she lived a million and ten miles away, I say.

Not a million, she answers, looking at dirty underwear instead of me.

I love Grandma, I say.

And she loves you.

Who does she look like?

She's an older woman, Charlie. She looks like—

I said *who*, not *what*.

She stops. You mean—?

Does *she* have freckles?

The questions you ask!

Are her eyes the same as yours and mine?

Help me put the soap in, replies Mom, lifting me up onto the machine. She knows I love putting the soap in; she thinks I'll forget about Grandma Ruthie. Next to the machine is a hole in the floor that is full of water. The water is flat and freezing, but I bet there are eels down there. Eels and biting fish and sea monsters. Dad calls the hole a pump. Mom calls it a menace. They have to lock the washing room so we don't fall in. That's what they say, at least. The real reason for the lock is what lives in the furnace room next to it. A thing that growls and goes *hmmm* at night. My bedroom is right above the furnace room. Right above the thing.

See something in the sub-pump?

No, I answer, jumping down.

I see an accident waiting to happen, says Mom.

I help her carry the basket up the stairs. We always fold laundry in the kitchen.

Santa comes to the house on Christmas Eve, right?

While we're all sleeping, she replies.

And he leaves loads of gifts for good boys and girls?

Boys and girls don't need loads of gifts. A few nice ones will do.

I practise my next question before asking it.

Your lips are moving, says Mom. This must be important.

Santa has to do a lot of preparations, doesn't he? He must make his list of who is naughty and who is nice *way* before Christmas.

She is silent.

There's no way he can change his mind at the last minute, is there?

What do you mean?

Even if a kid does something a little naughty, a little bad, a few days before Christmas, he'll still get the presents he asked for?

She reaches out, as if to touch my forehead again, but changes her mind. That frown, she says.

Won't he?

Santa's sled is packed with toys, answers Mom. He can't change his mind now.

I nod.

How *was* school this morning?

I can't tell her. Not that. But then I look at her and she looks at me. At her son. At her big boy.

I tell her everything.

I'll see Grandma Ruthie on Sunday and she may look like me or Puss or Mom, and I'll probably see Grandpa at his farm next summer, whenever that is, and he may look like me as well, but I've never seen my other grandma or grandpa and I won't ever see them, except up in heaven, when who knows what any of us will look like. (Angels are all white.) Grandmothers and especially grandfathers are old people whose kids aren't kids anymore and who don't live with them in their houses. When they die, grandparents fly up to heaven to sit with God and the angels. Everyone misses them but no one calls them back. Moms and dads, though, are different. They can't stay in heaven. They can't be dead for longer than a cup of tea, a few minutes alone on the couch. We need them here, because we're children, and they need to be here, because they're parents. That's called a family. That's called a home.

1966

CHARLIE:
A CAUTIONARY TALE

Prologue

There once was a boy named . . .

Me. Charlie Foran. In *Pierre,* by Maurice Sendak, the boy
doesn't care about anything and has to learn a moral,
which Mom says is a life lesson. In my life I care about
learning to read and write. Words and sentences and pairs-
of-graphs: books without pictures, books Toad calls stupid.
In two weeks I start Grade One with Missus Nolan, whose
room is next to the kindergarten. Missus Nolan teaches
children the twenty-six sounds called the alphabet; she
teaches how to use letters to make words and how to use

words to make sentences. Sentences are thoughts you want people to read, not hear. Writing lets you talk without moving your lips.

Sipping once, sipping twice, says my favourite book, *sipping chicken soup with rice.* But can I spell *chicken*? Read the word *rice*? *That Sam-I-am: do you like green eggs and ham?* But can I write *eggs* for the one-eyed messes we eat at breakfast? See *green* and know it's the colour of grass? I'm tired of pretending to read books to Mom or Toad or just myself. Tired of saying sentences from memory while turning the pages. Tired of asking Mom how to spell my name—*See-Aych-Eh-Are-Elle-Eye-Ee*—and repeating it back, and her replying, Good, now you can spell. No I can't spell, Mom. No I can't read or write.

Once I can do these things, I'll give Toad my picture books. Dr. Seuss and Maurice Sendak. *Goodnight, Moon* and *Little Bear.* Here, I'll say. Take them. When I was a kid, I liked these too.

That's what I care about. Mom, who is explaining that *Pierre* is divided into chapters—she points at a page, though all I can see are the numbers—says I need to tell everyone what I don't care about, so we can begin the story. Maybe a friend? she suggests. A best friend who you're not getting along with?

Oh yes: I ask her about the word *cautionary.* You're a careful soul, she answers. No need for this to be a cautionary tale.

Chapter 1

One day, his mother said . . .

Outside for a while. I've housework to do, and can't always be talking to you.

Much obliged, I say from the door.

Got my coonskin hat on my head and my rifle over my shoulder. *Davy*, I sing, *Davy Crockett, / King of the wild frontier.* At every driveway I stop and take aim. Pow! I say, scaring birds from trees. Shot me a critter. Pow! A fuzzy-wuzzy bear.

Hey there, Davy, says Missus Myers on her front steps. She's cutting roses with scissors.

Ma'am, I reply.

Playing with Pete today?

He's in the ditch.

I can see that. And have you invited him to play Davy Crockett with you?

Funny: Mom asked the same question at breakfast. Davy Crockett is a game for one kid only, I answer. Unless Pete wants to be a possum.

Grade One starts soon, doesn't it?

Two weeks.

Too bad you and Pete go to different schools. I know he's sad about it.

Pete isn't Catholic, I reply. George is. And I have a friend named Jimmy who lives in Ireland. We'll all be back at BTS.

She looks past me to our house. I know she's watching

Pete and hoping he can't hear what we say. When Missus Myers smiles, it's probably because Pete has waved at her. Don't shoot the Wardens' cat, okay? she says, waving back.

Davy Crockett would never shoot a cat, I answer. He's king of the wild frontier.

She asks about our summer holiday.

Great, I tell her, tipping my hat again.

My Blind River cousins talked in English with me and in French with their parents. In English, they said *geez* and *fuckin-eh* and hollered *tabernac!* when they jumped off swings. They used *weener* and *dick* for penis and *china* for the thing girls hide up their bums. My cousins also spat between their teeth and squished every bug on the sidewalk and played cowboys and Indians up the hill behind town. Luc, who is eight, said he knew a spot I'd want to see, because I was a city kid from *down south*. It was a hole in the earth, wider than our sub-pump, with grass growing over the rim and a black centre. Luc hawked into the hole and shouted *fuckin-eh*, the spit dropping into the dark. What is it? I asked, stepping back. An old mindshaft, he answered. Fall in, and next thing you know you're eating chop suey with Chinamen.

Pete is in the ditch. His hands are behind his head and his shoes are off. He chews a piece of grass.

What's in your pocket? I ask him.

Stuff.

Show.

You first.

No, you.

He and I have been here all summer and we've run out

of things to do. Adults walk past, but usually the same adults at the same time. Mister Smith with his lunch pail and work boots. Mister Kiley with his briefcase and black shoes. Even talking with old Graham Nester and his dog Robert-the-Bruce—*Cull the wee pooch Rroby, bays*, Graham told me and Pete—isn't a thrill anymore. Neighbourhoods aren't adventures. They aren't the wild frontier or the Ten-Acre Wood or even the Bumpity. Allan goes by on his bike. He always looks as if he's rolled in dirt. His hair is brush-cut and toes poke through his runners. He doesn't smile or say hi. All he does is shout: Never reveal the secret code!

He's strange, I say.

Weird, agrees Pete.

We watch him disappear into the Bumpity.

What have you got?

Pennies crushed by trains, I answer. You lay them on the tracks and wait for a train to pass. Then you scrape them loose. My cousins showed me.

I'd hate to get crushed by a train.

It'd break your bones.

But words will never hurt me, adds Pete.

I keep quiet.

I got a worm, he says, patting his pocket. Squishy and disgusting against my leg.

My dad says this: when Pete Nicolson grins, his smile pushes his ears even farther out. His parents are talking about an operation. Doctors will break the bones behind the ears so they'll flop down, like on other kids. Mom tells me not to make Dumbo jokes around him.

Show, I say.

You first.

No, *you* first.

At lunch I explain to Mom what happened. She's buttering bread at the counter. Puss is in the backyard with Toad. Pete lied about having a worm in his pocket, I tell her, and when I said he was a liar he called me a name and now he's not my friend anymore.

You didn't—?

He called me Freckles.

What did we talk about, Charlie?

But he—

Does the name Freckles really hurt your feelings?

Yes, I answer in a voice that sometimes flies out my mouth. When she doesn't answer, I kick the floor. It *does*, I repeat.

You know how sensitive Pete is about his ears. He's your best friend. You should—

Toad is eating dirt again, shouts Puss from the yard.

I'm disappointed in you, says Mom, crossing to the door.

You're a bad mom.

Stop that.

Saying those things hurts *my* feelings, I reply. Parents aren't supposed to be mean to their children. They aren't supposed to make them cry.

Go draw a picture.

And you don't even care that my teeth are falling out!

She wants to say more—I want her to speak one soft word, so I can apologize and give her the special Blind River kiss—but she also has to watch Toad. Mike, calls Mom from the porch, you're going to make yourself sick . . .

In my room I draw a boy standing in a field of flowers. The boy is smiling and the flowers are smiling as well. I colour the hair black for bad and the face red for embarrassment and the smile yellow for being sorry. The flower I colour pink for her, and also because it *is* her—a pink rose. I ask Puss to write some words on the drawing. She makes me cry by saying I must still be a kid, since I can't write my own notes, but then she feels ashamed. The note says: DEAR MOM. I KNOW YOU WANT TO BE A GOOD MOM. I KNOW YOU CARE. I STILL LOVE YOU. SIGNED, YOUR SON, CHARLIE (SAM WINKIE) FORAN. My sister scrunches her nose when I ask her to put some gross becks at the bottom. What are those? she says. Blind River kisses, I answer. She scrunches again. XXX, she writes. OOO. Not those things, I complain. Gross becks!

In the afternoon Mom asks me to play with Toad. Let him play hide-and-seek with you kids, she says. I need to vacuum the house.

Want to kill some ants, Toad? I ask.

Squish, he answers.

Play hide-and-seek, repeats Mom. Just for an hour.

Pete is sitting on his lawn. I wave him across to the ditch. We have to play hide-and-seek with Toad, I say.

Puss and Toad and George's sister Jodi show up. My turn comes to be It. Toad stands with me under the weeping willow tree.

Go hide with the others, I tell him.

He runs away.

One—two—three—four—five, I count loud and clear. Six–seven–eight–nine–ten, I say, only peeking a little. Everyone is already hidden. Eleventwelvethirteenfourteen fifteensixteenseventeen . . . eighteen . . . nineteen . . . TWENTY! I turn and sing: Ready or not, here I—

I run into him.

I hiding, he says.

Where?

Hind you.

Spaz, I say.

Toad starts to cry so I push him. He falls accidentally to the pavement and cries louder.

Mom steps out. She sighs when I tell her what happened. Toad stays on his bum.

Sorry, Toad, I say quietly.

Bad brother, he answers.

No way anyone is hiding in the Macgreevys' yard. (They put children into pork pies.) No way anyone has gone beyond the Campbells'. Backyards are out of bounds. Garages have to be open to count. I check the bushes of Floyd-the-garbageman, who shares our driveway. A row of trees separates his house from the Smiths'. Nothing there either. Across the street, Missus Myers has trees and bushes and flower beds. In the laneway between her house and the Nicolsons' are grapevines. The grapes are purple and taste sweet, once you peel away the sour skins.

Come out, come out, wherever you are, I shout.

We can't, answers Pete. We're hiding.

I knew he'd answer. I also knew he'd be in the bushes below Missus Myers' front window. His runners are red. His knees aren't green.

Fee, fi, fo, fum, says the bush. I smell the poo of a big fat bum.

The stinky poo, I say.

The smelly turds.

I smell stinky poo and smelly turds and—

More bathroom talk, boys? asks Missus Myers from her porch.

Pete said it first.

Did not.

Did so.

It doesn't matter, she says. Just try to use nicer words, okay?

That was *your* fault, I tell him once we're back on the street.

Puss walks down from the Campbells'. 'Gross becks' isn't even real English, she says in her mean-sister voice.

That night I dream I slip into a tree trunk in Parkview Park. There should be a hiding place in the trunk. Instead I fall down a tunnel and land, thump, on a bed of carrots and lettuce. A rabbit nudges me. What are you doing in my house? it asks. Every time I try to climb out, I slide back. The rabbit says I'd better dig. Dirt covers my hair and chokes my mouth. At last I poke my head up. Far away I see the swings and slide and the rocket ship. Close by are flashlights firing beams. Adults searching the dark. My parents calling my name.

You're a rose, Mom, I say to Leo and Sylvester, the only two cuddlies left alive. A beautiful pink rose.

Chapter 2

*H*is father said . . .

Maybe the tooth will fall out today, Charlie. That way, you can show it to Grandpa this weekend.

Want to feel it?

I'm late, he says, getting into the car. He rolls down the window. Going to play with Pete?

I guess so.

He's a great kid. Your best friend, right?

Sure, Dad.

He gives me a Dad look. It says: Help me think of something else to say to you. Talking to him this way is weird. Normally, he is in front of me in the car and I can stare at the back of his neck, his combed hair. That's mostly how I see my dad: behind the driving wheel, leaning over me in bed, carving wood while listening to TV.

Got to go, he finally says. The engine roars. Don't kill too many bugs, okay? he adds, backing up.

Mom already talked to me at breakfast. Ants and beetles won't bite you, she said. Leave them be. Mosquitoes and blackflies will, I answered. Remember in Blind River? Most insects are harmless, Charlie. They don't deserve to die. I thought about this. Did your mom and dad deserve to die? I asked her. No one does, she replied. Were they bad people? They were wonderful, she said. Did they have old bodies with yucky skin and bones that kept breaking? My mother was sick before she died, she answered quietly. But no, they weren't very old. Mom had been looking at me, but then she turned away. I walked around the table so I could see her face again. Then I rubbed her forehead, tracing the lines with my fingers. Her skin was soft and smooth. Her bones felt strong. I won't kill anymore, I said to her. Promise.

There's an ant crawling up your arm, says Pete, flopping in the ditch.

I don't care.

What happens when it reaches your neck?

I don't care.

And crawls onto your face?

I promised my mom—

And slips up your nose or into your ear?

I crush the ant into smear.

Guess, says Pete.

A ball?

Nope.

A rock?

It's alive.

I look down at the pockets of his shorts. He's not lying this time.

A bird? I ask.

Toad, he answers.

He's in the house.

No he isn't, says Pete. From his pocket he pulls out a

real frog. It has marble eyes and a sad mouth and a heart that thump thumps through its chest.

My dad says it's a toad, he explains.

I let the toad hop up my shirt. It stops at my neck and stares at me. Thump thump goes its heart. Blink blink goes its eyes.

Some kids at our cottage run over toads with their bikes, says Pete.

Do they squish them?

Splat, he answers. Blood and guts. Smears of it.

Are the kids older?

Eight or nine.

My cousin Luc told me about boys in Blind River who blow up frogs with firecrackers, I say. He says that gunk flies everywhere.

You squish ants and beetles.

So?

Nothing, says Pete.

That makes me angry and I stand up. As I do, I glance at the ant smear on my arm. Pete is too busy letting the toad hop into the drain hole to notice.

Why'd you do that? I ask.

He shrugs.

I'd better go sit in Floyd's ditch, I say.

Floyd-the-garbageman's ditch is filled with rotting leaves and pebbles. The drain is clogged with candy wrappers and bits of gum, some showing teeth marks. I feel inside my mouth, just in case.

We lie on our bellies and whisper into the drain. We

hold spitting contests and do bathroom talk. Both of us wonder if Allan will ride past; neither of us speaks when four older boys roar by on three-speeds. Mom cooks hamburgers. Missus Nicolson brings out cake. Shining flashlights into the drain is spooky; it gets dark, and I start to shiver.

Better come in for the night, boys, says Dad.

Mister Nicolson blocks each exit with a board. The toad will be there for you in the morning, he promises.

We're going to my grandpa's farm tomorrow.

Shoot, says Pete.

Not until after lunch, adds my dad quickly. You kids can play together until then.

In bed I tell Toad about the toad. He listens so quietly I ask if he's still awake. His only answer is a sob. Then my brother calls for his mom. She demands an explanation. Toad, who can still barely talk, says some words. They're stupid, but Mom believes him.

Into the kitchen, she tells me.

I sit at the table for hours while she makes Toad feel better. When she enters, she gives me a cruel stare. I cross my arms.

What did you say to your brother?

Nothing.

I'll get your father up from the basement, she says. Then you'll tell me.

No I won't.

Mom opens the door. Dave, she calls.

Okay, okay, I say.

What is it? Dad calls back.

Nothing.

I only told him that a toad got caught in the drain under our driveway, I begin. In the middle of the drain was a hole you could never climb out of and the toad fell into the hole and died there, lonely and blue, and it turned rotten and smelly and you *know* I wasn't talking about Mike!

Go apologize.

I should whack him instead.

Are you being smart with me?

I'm a smart kid.

She can't decide whether to shout or laugh. Last day of summer, she says with a sigh. Thank God.

Will Grandma Ruthie be at Grandpa's farm tomorrow? I ask her.

No, honey, she won't.

Will someone else be there instead?

Goodnight, Charlie.

Isn't that weird—someone else where Grandma should be? Does she wear her clothes?

Does who?

The woman in Grandma's place.

Goodnight, she says again.

In the morning Dad asks if we're having toads-in-the-hole for breakfast. One toad in the culvert, he says, ruffling Toad's hair, and another in a hole. *Dave,* says Mom. She makes each of us a toad-in-the-hole—fried bread with an egg in the middle—even though it isn't Sunday. I eat mine with syrup. Toad cries again and she tells him to go watch television.

Mom stops me at the front door. School will last all day

this year, she says. Pete is sad about that. Could you be especially nice to him today?

Sure, Mom.

Pete is already in the ditch. My side is open, he says, pointing to the drain. Come out, toad!

It has two hours to show up, I answer. Then we leave for my grandpa's farm and summer is over.

He sticks his head in the culvert. He has to be in here, he says, his voice small.

George walks down from his house. Behind him is the sound of horrible-things-being-done-to-a-sheep-with-a-fork (says Dad): Mister Campbell, practising the bagpipes. What are you doing? he asks.

Nothing, we both answer.

Pete blocks his ears. That music hurts, he says.

Poor sheep, I say.

George turns red. My dad marched in a parade last week, he tells us.

Was he wearing a dress? asks Pete.

A kilt, dummy.

They both stand up. I've seen boys fight before, in the schoolyard or down at the Bumpity, but never friends and never in our neighbourhood.

Bet you guys can't name all the families on the block, I say, getting up fast.

Easy, says George.

Double easy, says Pete.

Start at Longmore, I say. On the other side.

Wilsons.

Jordans.

My house.

The Myerses and the Wardens and the Jakeses.

Your house and the Joneses and the fireman . . . What's his name?

Mister Grimly.

And then the Kileys and then the Bumpity and then . . .

And then . . .

Allan-the-ghost-boy! we shout together.

We trade names up our side of the street as well. I get the Macgreevys. They put children into pork pies, I add.

My dad is taking me to the legion hall for a party, says George. Only members and their families are allowed. He turns to leave. Want to walk to school together on Tuesday? he asks me.

I nod.

Pete gets that look on his face again. I wish I could go to school with you, he says. I wish I was Catholic.

It's not that great.

Yes it is.

If you're Catholic, I say, you have to stand behind the piano all morning.

That's not so bad.

And you get whacked on the knuckles by a principal who's a penguin.

Really?

And when you turn seven, I say, saving the best for last, they make you eat Jesus' body and drink his blood every Sunday.

Gross!

Disgusting, I agree.

He feels better, I can tell.

You're still my best friend, you know, I say.

Not George?

George is okay, I answer, thinking for the first time in ages about Jimmy Reilly. How long does a summer last? Long enough to almost forget about your new best friend. My tooth is going to fall out any second, I say to Pete. Want to feel it?

The toad! he replies.

Where?

He just hopped out of the drain. Then he hopped back in.

I press my face to the opening. The air smells like a toilet. Before long, I can't see a thing.

Stick your hand in, says Pete.

All I feel is slime and ooze. But then I touch something awful and pull back, scraping my arm. The sting stings. The scrape is pink.

Joked you!

I call him a name.

Mom, I say in the kitchen, my hand is probably broken and my arm is probably infected and we'd better go to the hospital right away because it's my left arm, the one I'm going to write words with, and, oh yeah, I hate Pete.

Tell me you didn't—

His ears *do* stick out the sides of his head, I say. He *is* a Dumbo.

Suddenly she laughs.

Pete can lie about the toad, I shout, and Dad can say toad-in-the-hole all he wants, but everything *I* do is wrong and bad, and that's why I hate Pete and Toad and I think you and Dad are the worst parents and I don't CARE if good boys shouldn't say such things.

Go to your room.

The worst parents in the—

To your—

I go to my room. There, I think up a note to give Mom, using brave and true words and bunches of gross becks. I keep hoping that Puss will knock on the door and offer to write it out. (She *knows* what a gross beck is. She was in Blind River too.) When she doesn't, I draw another picture. Mom comes in to pack our suitcase and I give her the drawing.

Usually you draw trains or rocket ships, she says. What made you decide to try a flower?

You did, I think to myself.

Chapter 3

*N*ow, *as the night began to fall . . .*

Spacegirl Puss and Spaceman Sam Winkie realized that Spaceman Toad's ship wasn't working right. Spaceman Sam Winkie said to Spacegirl Puss: I bet he got his ship from the planet Saturn, where they make cheap ships that can't survive a trip around the sun. If Spaceman Toad tries to make the voyage, he'll burn up like toast!

Don't scare them, says Mom.

Is this going to take much longer? asks Puss.

So Spaceman Toad's brother and sister, who cared about him very much, decided to catch Toad before he got too near the sun, says Dad. *Vroom*, they blasted away from the earth. *Vroom*, they came up to Mars. Once they were beside his ship, they flashed their blinkers and honked their horns.

Honk, honk, says Toad.

Dave, says Mom. Don't let him—

Want to honk the horn, Toad?

Yeah!

It's not safe.

Dad pulls Toad over the top of the seat and snuggles him between his legs. Toad pushes the horn and laughs. Honk, honk! he shouts.

Crawl over to your mother now.

He flings himself on her. Mike! she says, but lets him sit in her lap and bang on the dashboard.

Finally, Spacegirl Puss and Spaceman Sam Winkie got Toad's attention, says Dad. Pull over to that asteroid, called Sam Winkie. Once they landed, Puss and Sam Winkie explained to Toad that he needed a better spaceship to circle the sun. They said they knew where he could get one, and together they flew back to the earth. Know where Toad found the perfect spaceship?

Eaton's? asks Puss.

Parkview Park, answers Dad. That ship was just waiting for an adventure. Spaceman Toad rushed right up to it, climbed aboard and said—

Blast off! says Toad.

Blast off! repeats Dad. For the sun. Spacegirl Puss and Spaceman Sam Winkie were proud of their little brother and happy to help him. They decided to go along because they knew that a family made the best team in the galaxy.

Good story, Dad, I say.

B-O-R-I-N-G, spells Puss.

Don't be mean to Dad, I tell her.

I wasn't, she answers. I was just spelling his name for him.

Oh.

Want me to spell yours?

Sure.

S-T-U-P-I-D, whispers Puss.

I know we're at the farm even before Dad turns onto a dirt road and pebbles start to jump up underneath the car. My body tells me we've arrived. I don't feel sick, just weak. I also need to pee so badly I won't make it to a toilet, no matter how hard I pinch my penis.

Everyone gets out, except me. I sink down in the back-seat and hope maybe they'll forget—

Where is he? asks a roaring voice.

Around here somewhere, answers Mom.

Charlie, says Dad. Come and—

I step out.

You're the one with my name, aren't you? he roars again. I don't remember saying you could borrow it.

I smile at him. I also keep my legs crossed. Mom, I whisper. Help me . . .

Shake my hand, Charlie Foran, says my Grandpa. Show me how grown-up you are now.

He has wet silver hair and a moustache. His voice is so grumbly that birds probably shoot from trees, especially when he laughs. His hand is huge and his shake hurts. His smell, which Dad calls col-own, makes me woozy.

I'd better take him inside, says Mom.

Come in the house, everyone, announces Grandpa. Shirley has some sandwiches ready.

Good to see you, Dad, says my dad.

The weekend goes like this:

1. Shirley, whose hair is golden but whose voice is a growl, serves us sandwiches and milk.
2. Give you a penny for every fly you catch, says Grandpa to all of us.
3. Farm dogs yap.
4. Grandpa shows us the horses in his barn. They have massive brown bodies but skinny black legs. When Grandpa pulls back a horse's lips to show us its teeth—so huge and puke-yellow I decide I don't want my own to fall out—the horse nods its head and says, *Heeeh!*
5. I step in manure. That's horse shit, says Puss to me. Mom cleans my shoes in the sink.
6. Shirley serves us hamburgers and potato salad. She brushes against me at the table. Her scent—of cigarettes and even stronger col-own than Grandpa's—makes me

certain she stole Grandma's clothes, probably out of her closet.

7. Just eat what's on your plate, says Mom in a low voice. Please.

8. Grandpa lets me fire his pellet gun. The gun is black and heavy. I shoot once into the woods and then give it back. He loans me his handkerchief to wipe my hands. The hankie is soft and has letters on it.

9. The bedsheets smell like baby powder.

10. A clock—*tick tock, tick tock*—keeps me awake. Toad can't sleep either. I ask if he wants to share my bed. He kicks all night.

11. I wake up suddenly. *Pow!* Got me one. *Davy, Davy Crockett* . . . My mouth is dry.

12. Shirley serves us eggs and toast. The eggs are runny and I think, maybe for the first time ever, about them being dead chickens. I eat the eggs anyway. So does Puss. Toad makes a face so Mom eats his.

13. I bring Grandpa a Kleenex full of flies. These were already dead when you found them, weren't they? he says. When I nod, he roars and says, No deal, kid. I run away crying.

14. Mom finds me behind a chair in the living room. Don't make me give my name back, I tell her. I haven't even learned how to read or write it yet!

15. Shirley shakes Mom's hand. Also Dad's. Give Shirley a hug, children, says Mom.

16. I shake Grandpa's hand again. You can keep it for now, he says, his laugh another rumble. Winking at me, he

slips something into my palm. One dollar, says Dad outside. One Canadian dollar with the Englishman's queen on it.

In the car Mom asks us to sing songs. When no one does, she asks me to tell the story of *Pierre*. It's a book, Mom, I answer. I need to look at it to speak the words.

Can't you remember a little?

Maybe, I say. But without the pictures, I can't remember much. One part comes into my head, along with a drawing of a lion. Is that all you have to say? I read from memory. *I don't care.* Then I'll eat you, if I may. *I don't care.* So the lion ate Pierre.

Very nice, says Mom.

Dad doesn't sing or tell a story and Mom keeps running her hand through his hair. Twice she asks him if he's okay. Twice he answers, Fine. We stop at a restaurant for hot dogs and french fries.

Chapter 4

Arriving home at six o'clock . . .

Actually, school finishes way before supper. I stand near Missus Nolan's desk on the first morning of class. Above the blackboard are two photographs. One is of a woman wearing a dress and crown. The other is of a man, also in a dress, with a cap on his head and a cross around his neck.

He's the Pope, says a voice I know. I say hi to Jimmy
Reilly. Great to see him again. Great to see his freckles.

And she's the Queen, I answer. Her face is on a dollar
my grandpa gave me.

Did you know they were married?

Who?

The Pope and the Queen. Big wedding.

In Ireland? I ask.

You bet, he answers. They have ten children and twenty
grandchildren, plus two of each kind of animal. Their house
is a giant boat with a swimming pool.

And TV?

Colour, says Jimmy.

We snigger. Suddenly I remember last year and glance
around the room. We're safe: no piano anywhere.

Missus Nolan gives us desks. I'm near the front, Jimmy
is near the back. (George is in the other Grade One.) Our
teacher has honey hair and tinfoil skin. When she speaks
her voice is sweet; when she walks her dress swishes. For
sure, she has a newer body and nicer skin than Miss Malone.

It's going to be an exciting year, boys and girls, she
announces. We're going to learn to read and begin to
learn to write. See those letters running across the top of
the blackboard? That's our alphabet train. We'll ride it
every day.

Kids *oooh* in surprise, but I spotted the train the second
I walked in. It begins above the door, passes underneath the
Pope-Queen and runs into the far wall. First comes the
engine. Next is a letter with a drawing of an apple beneath

it—A. Then B with a buzzing bee and C with a car, which is weird: *kuh* not *see*. I count twenty-three more letters and pictures, and finally another train.

Want to ride the train right now? asks Missus Nolan.

Yes! I answer.

All aboard, she calls, raising her pointer. She hits each letter hard, *whack*, adding more black spots to the cards. A, shouts Missus Nolan (*whack*) . . . B (*whack*) . . . C (*whack*) . . . Join in, everyone! . . . D (*whack*) . . .

I should know the alphabet by tomorrow and be reading books in a week. How much longer until I can write my own notes? A month, maybe.

George is waiting by the steps to Bayview Avenue. His face changes when he sees Jimmy.

Want to go down to the ravine and spy on the older kids? Jimmy asks us.

Sure, says George.

I have to get home, I answer.

Why?

To tell my mom about the alphabet train.

Suck, says Jimmy.

I hide my hurt feelings. I'm surprised how strong they are. When Puss hurts me, I cry: if Toad tries to, I smack him. If Pete says anything mean, I let him know right away: if George does, I don't care.

We walk up Finch past the ravine. I keep both feet on the sidewalk. Jimmy tries to balance on the rail but slips off. The time he falls inside, landing at the top of the slope, he calls, Ahhhhh, I'm falling!

No doubt about it: he's wilder than I remember. What did you do all summer? I ask him.

Stayed up at our cottage mostly. Swam and caught frogs and built a beaver dam.

Did you squish the frogs?

What else? he says. But we didn't blow them up with firecrackers. Bigger kids do that.

Killing animals is cruel, says George.

Only if they're cats or dogs, replies Jimmy. The others don't feel pain.

I almost lost a tooth last week, I say. Mom is sure it won't hurt. Want to feel?

Jimmy sticks his finger in my mouth and wobbles the bottom tooth. George gives me an angry look and walks away.

What'd you do all summer? asks Jimmy.

Lay in a ditch with my friend Pete.

That's it?

We squished tons of bugs. Also we trapped a toad in a drain and, um, we watched him die.

Neat, he says.

We say goodbye at the crosswalk. George is waiting and we point our fingers. Want to touch the tooth now? I ask him once we're across.

Forget it, he replies.

Back at the house, I tell Mom about Missus Nolan and the alphabet train and Jimmy Reilly. I don't tell her about my lie, even though I feel strange.

Sounds like an exciting first day, she agrees.

Next week I'll read you *Pierre* and *Green Eggs and Ham*

using the words on the page. Won't that be incredible?

She smiles.

Actually, I add, I promised to give my old books to Toad once I learned to read. I'd better go get them.

Mom is pulling clothes from the washing machine. Why not wait a bit longer before giving Toad the books, she says. Just to be sure you're ready . . .

I lean over the pump hole.

Hello in there, I call.

That pump, she says with a sigh. I wish your father would cover it. She turns on the dryer. Go tell Pete about your day, Charlie. He should be home by now.

I cross to the Nicolsons'. His mom answers.

Tell Pete he can wiggle my tooth, I say.

Pete comes to the door. Your tooth is gross, he says.

Want to feel it?

Outside, orders Mrs. Nicolson.

Can we sit in the ditch? he asks on the front steps.

Why not?

You said we couldn't once summer was over.

I changed my mind.

At dinner Mom says she can't believe Pete and I had another fight. He put his finger in my mouth, I explain, but then he pulled back and said it was yucky. That wasn't very nice, I add, my face hot.

Afterwards I play alphabet train. *Choo choo,* I say, marching from the dining room into the kitchen.

Me play too, says Toad.

Forget it.

He can be the engine, says Mom.

I'm the engine, I answer.

Be the conductor instead. He announces all the letters. That's more important.

Off we march, Toad shouting *choo choo* and me calling A-B-C-D while riding from the hallway into the living room. We climb stairs. *Chug chug*, puffs Toad, out of breath. Sliding back down is the best. *Choo-oo-oo-oo*, he says. RR-SS-TT! I shout.

Puss walks behind us. You still can't spell your name, can you? she asks.

I started to learn today.

Do you know what day today is?

Friday?

Wrong.

Sunday?

Do you know what time it is?

After dinner?

That's not a time.

Two o'clock?

You can't read or write and you can't tell time or even guess what day it is, she says. You're just a—

But I *want* to be grown-up, I answer, tears pouring out my eyes. I want to!

She checks to see if Mom is watching. You will be soon, she adds in an almost-whisper. Don't worry.

I sob.

There, there, says Puss, patting me on the back. It's okay, baby.

Toad pats me on the back as well. Dere, dere, he says. Iz okay, baby.

Dad doesn't get home until late. I wait for him. The moment he enters, I smell his sweet pipe and stinky cologne. His hand is smooth on the outside but his palm is rough, his fingernails bumpy. He makes me think of Grandpa, though I know he isn't that old.

We have a special guest, he says.

Grandma Ruthie?

No, not Grandma, he answers after a silence. It's a surprise. You'll have to wait until morning.

I hear the sound of a hammer whacking nails. Next morning I know where to look for the guest. Toad follows me into the yard. The old rabbit pen has been fixed up: more wire and a door that locks. Inside the pen is a huge bird with skin flopping below its beak and eyes so small they'd get lost on a plate of peas.

Bach bach bach, says Toad.

It's too big for a chicken, I say.

Mom and Dad come out.

I don't know, Dave . . .

It was a gift from a contractor, he says. They raise animals in their backyards. I couldn't refuse it. Besides, Thanksgiving is only a month away.

If you think we're going to—

We won't talk about it now. He turns to me. What do *you* think, Charlie?

What is it?

Ham, says Toad.

Turkey, corrects Dad.

I can hardly wait to tell the guys.

Chapter 5

They rushed the lion into town . . .

Are lions left-handed? Who cares: *Pierre* is a book for kids. I barely remember the words anymore. I haven't read it the old way in ages.

Try holding your pencil in your other hand, says Missus Nolan on the last day before Thanksgiving.

Why?

Just try it.

Sliding the pencil between the finger and thumb is tough. I have no strength: I can't push down. Still, I start the letter A with my wrong hand, to please her. The lines are wobbly. None of them connect.

Lucky you were born when you were, says my teacher.

I am silent.

Try to be a little neater, okay?

Can I show you what I did during announcements?

Of course.

Mom printed my name on a pad last week using capitals, and I've been practising. This morning I wrote it without looking once. C H A R L I E, the letters say.

Am I the first kid in the class to do it? I ask Missus Nolan.

She touches my shoulder.

Sister Mary Wyatt walks into the room.

Stand up, class, says our teacher quickly.

The principal is dressed in black, except for the white trim around her face, and holds a string of beads, called a rose-mary, instead of a ruler. Sit down, please, she orders.

We sit.

Today is a special day, begins Sister Mary. This morning we celebrate Friday mass here at school for the first time this year. Father Ferguson will be joining us, and he has asked me to invite . . . Excuse me, Lenny Grusa. Excuse me, other naughty boy . . .

We all look. Billy Neary is the other naughty boy and he has turned pale. But Lenny Grusa, who has already been sent to the office twice, grins. Sister Mary Wyatt glares at him. She's right beside my desk. Her robe brushes the surface. Her spotted hand touches the wood.

. . . Father Ferguson has asked me to invite both Grade One classes to attend today's mass. You will have to sit quietly while the older children receive holy communion. Remember that Jesus Christ, our Lord and our Saviour, will be coming down from heaven to be with us. Remember that, boys and girls. Remember . . .

She stops. Her body stiffens. (I can feel it.) Her fingers jab at the desk. I don't dare look up at her. I barely dare to breathe.

Will *you* remember about Jesus, Lenny Grusa?

What? asks Lenny.

Into the hallway, says Sister Mary.

I didn't do—

Missus Nolan, please escort Mister Grusa outside.

Yes, Sister Mary Wyatt.

Our teacher takes Lenny by the arm. His cheeks and neck turn more purple than pink; she suddenly looks tired, not as young as before.

Where was I? asks the principal. Does anyone recall where I was?

She is talking to me now. I can feel it too, even though I'm staring at my desk. Did you write this? she asks, touching the pad.

Yes, Sister, I answer in the smallest voice ever to come out of my mouth.

Since you're so good with words, um, Charlie, ah yes, Charlie Foran—your sister Debbie is a lovely girl—you must remember where I was before Lenny Grusa decided to act smart.

You were telling us about Jesus coming down from heaven . . .

Of course, says Sister Mary Wyatt. When she smiles, her front teeth stick out and her top lip turns in. Her eyes are blue but watery; her nose is covered in spots. Jesus will be with us this morning, Grade Ones, she says. To help celebrate the mystery of the covenant. Even though you won't be sharing in that mystery for another year, our Lord will still be very, very interested in how you behave. Which boys and girls remain quiet and respectful during mass will be noticed. Noticed and remembered. By Jesus Christ *and* by me.

Thank you, Sister Mary, says Missus Nolan.

God bless, answers the principal.

Since the school gym hasn't been built yet, mass is held in an empty room. Our class is given two benches at the back. Squeeze in there, boys and girls, orders Missus Nolan. She sits in front of me and Jimmy Reilly. During mass, I hear her sigh and watch her smooth her dress with her hand. I also notice how nice—still young, I guess—the skin is on her shoulders and arms. Young like my mom's; way younger and nicer than Sister Mary Wyatt's. (Miss Malone's is the worst by far.) I bet Missus Nolan is disappointed that Lenny Grusa acted bad. I bet she's embarrassed. Besides thinking about my teacher, I study the clock on the wall and the photos of the Pope-Queen. I even wiggle my tooth with my tongue. Each wiggle makes a sucking sound.

An old priest stands and kneels and kneels and stands. Two big kids in angel outfits pour water into cups and ring bells. The rest of us answer questions and say prayers while standing and kneeling and then standing again. Once in a while we sit; once in a while we sing. Jimmy keeps his hands pressed into a steeple, left thumb over right, and repeats all the prayers. His face is white and hair sticks to his forehead. He keeps staring at a spot above the altar.

Jesus is coming down from heaven, he whispers to me. He's coming!

Shh, says Missus Nolan.

I'm not ready to see Jesus, says Jimmy. I'm scared to see him.

Our teacher turns around. Quiet, boys, she says. Then she looks at Jimmy: Are you all right?

He shakes his head.

Want to leave?

Jesus will notice, whispers Jimmy.

Sister Mary Wyatt, near the front, also turns around. She stares at me—not fair.

Come, says Missus Nolan.

They leave.

I search the schoolyard at lunch. He stands by himself in the parking lot. From the driveway we can see the almost-ready church across Bayview Avenue. I capture it between my praying hands. Here is the church, I say to Jimmy, and here is the steeple. Here is the priest—I wag my baby finger—and here are the people!

Later he walks home with me and George to look at the turkey. What kind of a name is Ham? asks Jimmy.

My brother thought of it, I reply. He's two.

We enter the Bumpity from Dunforest Avenue. Tree branches bend in the wind. Leaves flutter down onto our heads.

Get sticks, says George.

Why? asks Jimmy.

We're going to hunt the Box Man.

Maybe I should go find Pete, I say. He loves doing that.

No time, answers Jimmy. Once the Box Man realizes we're after him, he'll run away.

We find sticks and start to whack bushes and chop the heads off plants.

Take that, Box Man!

George beats a tree branch and small birds shoot up. I

whack a plant and almost get stung by a wasp. Jimmy disappears behind the tallest bushes in the Bumpity. We call his name. George and I fight branches and leaves to the spot where we sometimes find empty bottles. Jimmy stands next to a real box. On its cardboard side is a drawing of a washing machine; sticking out of its mouth is a blanket.

I'm not going in, says George.

Me neither.

I'll go, says Jimmy.

He tells us what he finds: two socks and a shoe, a pack of cigarettes and matches, a magazine. For ages after that, he says nothing and doesn't come out. I walk around the back of the box to make sure it isn't a magic wardrobe.

You okay? I call.

The magazine has pictures, he answers.

What kind of—?

Jimmy crawls out. This time his face is pink and his freckles are glowing. His eyes are also wild again. He looks first at me and then at George. Box Man, he shouts. He's coming to get us!

Boy, do we run.

Who's your friend? asks Mom in the backyard.

Hello, Missus Foran, says Jimmy.

And where does your family live, Jimmy?

I am about to answer: *In Ireland, Mom: I already told you.* But he replies, Pemberton Avenue.

That's not far at all, she says.

Once she's gone inside, Jimmy and George make fun of Ham.

Good with mashed potatoes, says Jimmy, poking his finger through the wire.

He's a pet, I explain.

And gravy, adds George.

Ham isn't for eating, I say to them. We've already told my dad that.

Next day is Saturday. (I can tell by all the cartoons on TV.) Mom takes me, Puss and Toad out for ice cream. It's too cold to eat ice cream so we have doughnuts and hot chocolate instead. Puss eats more of her own hair than her doughnut. Mom keeps stirring her coffee. I ask if something is wrong and when she doesn't answer I rub her forehead and say, Do you remember? For some reason I keep my hand there—I like touching my mom, smelling my dad—and flatten my palm across her brow, the way she does to check my temperature. I promise not to kill any more bugs, I say. And this time I *really* mean it. Okay, says Mom with a sigh. (I don't think she even heard what I said.) We can probably go home now.

You don't know what's going on, do you? says my sister in the car. As soon as Mom stops in the driveway, Puss flies out the door and races into the backyard. I catch up and see that the pen is empty. By then, though, she has moved on to the kitchen.

Where *is* he? she's asking Dad.

Calm down.

Where?

Moo, says Dad. Help me calm this—

Debbie says that Dad killed Ham. Twice: You killed him! She runs up the stairs. Then she runs back down.

What have you done with Josy?

She's a cat, answers Dad. I wouldn't—

Hearing her name, Josy tiptoes into the kitchen, the way cats do.

Poor kitty! says Puss, diving on her. Josy squirms but my sister still picks her up. *Don't* eat Josy, she says.

Jesus H. Christ, says Dad.

Stay out of the downstairs bathroom, children, orders Mom, taking a pail from under the sink.

Soon Puss is bawling and Toad is bawling and I'm bawling too, even though I don't care. Sad, though. Poor Ham. Poor turkey. Dad refuses to show us the body. He won't even say where it is. Puss keeps glancing at the fridge, as if the door is going to swing open and a headless Ham will pop out. Mom and Dad argue about something. I won't do it, Dave, she says. I just can't.

I check the fridge when no one is looking. I check all the cupboards and closets as well. In the basement I open the dryer door and look into the sink. I even jiggle the water in the sub-pump in case a dead turkey floats to the surface. The furnace room door is closed. If I was braver I'd check in there. But the monster is already back—I heard the *hmmm* the other night for the first time since last winter—and besides, I can't reach the light-bulb string.

The *hmmm* wakes me up in the night. Toad? I call. You asleep?

He doesn't answer.

Ham is underneath your bed, Toad, I say. Dad hid the

body there. He's oozing blood and guts. His head is chopped off. Why don't you check?

All my brother does is snore. Just as well: even making up those words puts bumps on my arms. I need to pee, but decide to wait. Instead I spell my name in my head. It comes out wrong. That makes me angry and I jump up and cross to my desk. The light stings my eyes. I close them, open them, close them again. They stop hurting and I find a blank page of my pad.

I write C and then A. Wait, I forgot the H. H goes before A: I put it in. The letters aren't perfect—A is a tent, hard—but okay. Next I do the E. That letter is tough and I erase it twice. What comes after? R, I think, or maybe L. I hear myself say *ooooh* and I hear Toad mumble, but I decide to start over. C A H I, I write. No, no, no. C H A E L. No, no, no.

Toad calls for his mom.

Shh, I tell him. I'm writing.

He calls again.

What on earth . . . ? asks Mom in the doorway.

I can't write my name, I say. I'll never be able to write my name again!

She calms me down. Can I give you a gross beck? I ask her in bed. I guess so, she answers, her forehead wrinkling. When I kiss her on both cheeks, Blind River style, Mom smiles a big smile and says, *Un gros bec!* How silly of me. Like *tante* Marie does, I explain.

For Thanksgiving we eat soup and buns, mashed pota-toes and corn, plus ham. Mom had one in the freezer that she cooked using pineapples. The ham once had eyes and ears and even teeth. The ham once snorted and maybe burped. Dad knows it and Mom knows it and so does Puss. (Toad hasn't a clue.) I eat five slices. The only thing weird is the taste the ham leaves in my mouth: salty, bitter.

Fine, says Dad once the table has been cleared. I'll get some bunnies for the pen tomorrow.

Hooray, says Toad.

Okay, says Puss, her eyes still red.

Mmm, I say, letting an awful joke out of my head. I bet bunny stew is delicious.

Dad howls.

Charles Foran, calls Mom.

Bunny hash, says Dad.

I'm going to be sick, says Puss.

Puke, adds Toad.

Bunnies-on-toast, I say.

Bunnies-in-the-hole, says Dad, who's the best.

Pete knocks on the door after dinner. It's nearly dark out but Mom says we can play in the front yard. Put a jacket on, she tells me. *Et donne-moi un gros bec, cher enfant,* she adds. What? I answer her. What are you saying in French?

Got anything in your pocket? asks Pete in the yard.

Only a tissue.

Me too.

We are quiet.

What did you have for Thanksgiving? I say.

Turkey.

We had ham.

Poor bird, says Pete. He walks to the ditch. Want to? he asks.

I am about to say no—the ditch is covered in wet leaves—but then I look at Pete. He is wearing his best clothes and a new jacket. His shoes are shiny brown.

Sure, I answer.

The ground is cold and I can feel the wet in my pants. Pete puts his hands behind his head.

Better not take off your shoes, I say, my words making clouds.

The toad! he answers.

I glance at the mouth of the drain. I even laugh, because he does.

There's no Box Man, is there? asks Pete.

I saw a real box down at the Bumpity. Someone lives in it, I think.

My last sentence must sound funny, because my tooth isn't loose anymore: it's floating in my mouth. I spit it into my hand. Blood, I say, remembering how the ham tasted. Yuck.

The tooth fairy will come tonight.

My sister gets ten cents a tooth, I say, the words slushy and gooey. (*My shishr gez hen thens a woosh.*)

Want to go to the store tomorrow?

Pete's ears stick out and he has a goofy grin. We used to hold each other's penises. He's my best friend.

Sure, I answer again.

We lie in the ditch getting more cold and more wet. The tooth is warm in my fist. Only when I feel it jab into my skin do I open my hand. I ask Pete if he wants to hold it. He says yes.

This is my body, I tell him.

Oh yes: the moral of *Charlie* is: Never name your turkey Ham. (No! says Mom. The moral is: Friends are important.)

1967

Kids who aren't to blame squeeze into fridges and freezers they find in backyards and down in ravines, and then pull the door shut. They forget about the devil. They forget about sin. I can picture them doing it. Decent boys, just a bit wild. I can see the boy—Jimmy Reilly, maybe—deciding that lying inside the freezer isn't exciting enough for a seven-year-old. Shut the door, and you've been locked in a treasure chest by pirates. Shut the door, and you've been buried in a coffin by ghouls and are going to have to say Chazam! and break out, the way Superman blasts walls and Batman busts chains. Only you really are in a fridge and Christ really was crucified, and the door was slammed and the nails were hammered, and soon you are going to cough and choke and beg, My God, My God, why have you—

You okay, Charlie?

Fine, I answer, blinking my eyes. (*Can't you see I'm trapped, Mom? Won't you help me?*)

He has the hiccups, says Puss.

No I don't, I tell her.

I'm in my proper place, I would say to my sister, *and even though I've done nothing wrong I know that if I hiccup one more time my brains are going to shoot out my ears and if Dad doesn't get rid of the furnace monster we're all going to die and, anyway, why does it matter which fingers I hold my pencil with?* But talking doesn't interest me. Sitting in my jacket and hat and pants and boots in my place—my proper place—does. Staying in my thoughts. Just being a kid. I always sit behind Dad. Toad, also called Mike, likes it in the centre, so he can stand on the hump and bug the parents. Debbie, who I stopped calling Puss the day she threatened to blab the name Sam Winkie all over the schoolyard, sits behind Mom, though she spends her time on the back window sill, waving at cars. I'm the middle kid, meaning I should be in the middle of the backseat, but I also need a window, especially in winter. Today is a perfect thinking day. Today I can write

Puss / Debbe

Sam Winkie / Charlie

Toad / Mike

real fast, so Debbie won't see what I've called her, and then erase it just as quick with my sleeve. If I'm in no hurry to think more, I wait for the glass to fog back up. If there's a rush, I blow hot breaths and it's ready. Anytime I want, I can wipe away what I've written: anytime Puss or Mom asks for a look, I smear the words—INRI, for sure—and say,

Whoops, sorry Deb, there's nothing to read. At least Dad won't ask about my window thinking. He's too busy driving us home in bad weather. His hair is still peach fuzz, especially the soft bristles at the back of his neck that I sometimes pet, making him laugh and say, Quit it! His arms are still freckly. He still sings cowboy songs—*Say, hey, good lookin' / what ya got cookin'*—and still drums on the steering wheel, even though I tell him *what ya* is bad English and Puss asks him to please stop hurting her ears. My ears hurt as well, but I figure cowboy songs are better than questions only Debbie can answer so far: what is the capital of New Brunswick? (That's a province, like Toronto.) Who was the first American president? (America is Niagara Falls. They're fighting Vietnam there.) Mom won't be reading my words today, either. She's too busy watching the highway, even though the air outside is the blur of a broken TV, and squinting with each squeak of the wipers. All she says is that the weather isn't bad, it's terrible. A blizzard, she adds, when Dad doesn't answer. A *mindshaft*, I would say, only no one would understand me. Think about it. We're on a highway somewhere between Grandma Ruthie's motel in a town called Minden and our house in a town called Willowdale. Maybe we're driving past gas stations with chip trucks and stores that sell Indian feathers. Maybe the countryside is nice to look at. Who can tell? Snow is falling and blowing and doing the same thing to my eyes that a switched-on light at night does. No sky above. No trees on the sides. Even the highway is only snaky lines made by car tires. Behind us is blur. Ahead of us is blur too, flakes splatting against the glass, the wind slipping through cracks. We're deep in a tunnel with only two dim red lights from a truck up ahead—Dad says that if we lose sight of the lights we're in trouble—to show the way.

Did you say something, honey? asks Mom.

Part of me wants to answer her—she's the only person who understands my thoughts—but I know I'm better off sinking into my jacket. The zipper is zipped so I can chew it and my cap is pulled so low the top half of everything is cut off, meaning most of what I hear is *blah blah blah*. I also wear mitts. I also stink so bad it's making me hiccup. Last September, when Puss and I got to miss a week of school so we could wish Canada a Happy Birthday in Montreal, I had on pants and a shirt. That meant I had to listen to her singing *Give me a place to stand and a place to grow* and to Toad shouting *Ontary-ary-ary-oh*, even when it wasn't the right moment in the song and even when Mom asked nicely if he could sing something else. We were pulling a tiny house behind us to sleep in at Expo, and I begged Dad to let me sit back there. He said the law forbade people from riding in the house while the car was moving. The law forbade! The way God forbids killing and stealing and coveting your neighbour's wife. (What does covet mean? asked Jimmy in Catechism. Not for children to understand, answered Father Ferguson, his jowls giggly. Only to obey.) Catholics—and I'm really one now: I ate my first communion last month—say *thee* and *thou* and other funny words. Our father ART, instead of IS, in heaven. You HAIL Mary, not say HI. THINE is the kingdom, which means IT'S

YOURS, GOD, I think. Catholics say these words during mass, when they're mumbling prayers or reading from the missile books, but afterwards they drink coffee and eat cookies and ask: How are you, son? and, Isn't the boy all grown-up now? I bet if someone were to ask, How art thou, son? you'd spit out your milk. I bet you would. Books are the same way. I read *Winnie the Pooh* and *The Tale of Peter Rabbit*. They were good, except the animals in the stories said *bother* and *bumbly* and put food in the *larder*, slipped off their *mackintoshes*. Mom looked puzzled by some of the words and said, Well, you know what they mean. Dad said these books were English and surely there had to be loads of Canadian or American books in the library. Pooh speaks with an English accent? Piglet talks like the Queen? I never knew that some books spoke English and others Canadian. (Toronto Canadian, I mean. Dad's language. Not Montreal's; not Mom's. When I was little, I didn't even understand that French had its own sounds and words. *Sur le pont d'Avignon*, Mom used to sing about a bridge where people danced. *On y danse, on y danse.* Also the jumping frog one: *La grenouille dans l'étang / Saute, saute!*). I never knew language was so complicated. I'd think about this more, only I want to concentrate on Grandma Ruthie today. She lives in a motel with her friend William, who definitely isn't our grandpa (Toad asked), and her eyes shine and she has to take medicine and go to bed early. *Sweetie pie*, she calls me. Also *sweetiekins*. Though I'm not sure what I want to think about her; Mom says thinking makes you know more stuff. I definitely want that with Grandma. She isn't like the grandmothers I see climbing the front porches of other houses on our street. She never knits sweaters. She doesn't bake cookies. Last summer Pete Nicolson said something mean about knowing a person. We were doing knock-knock jokes. His turn came. First he asked a question. Will you still know me in ten years? Sure, I answered. Okay, he said. Knock knock. Who's there? See, said Pete, you've forgotten me already! No I haven't, I answered. You're Pete. You're my best—

What's that about Pete? asks Mom.

Nothing, I answer, though I wouldn't mind finding out one or two things.

We really must visit the Nicolsons soon, she says. I've been meaning to call Elaine for ages.

You promised.

I meant it, honey.

He's just a sulk, says Puss.

Mom tells Dad that the weather is det-erior-ating, which sounds bad.

We're still better off driving than sitting on the shoulder, he answers.

Toad turns to me. Use your special powers, Charlie, he says.

What was I thinking about? Some thoughts get stuck—*Give me a place to stand*—in your mind, the way a roll of toilet paper blocks a toilet; others—*and a place to grow*—won't stay in there for more than a few seconds—*and call this land Ontario*—like dreams . . . *A place to stand, a place to*—

Stop!

We can't, says Dad. Look at that car in the ditch. It could easily be us.

He was talking to himself, Dad, says Puss.

Stupid songs are the toilet paper. Interesting thoughts about Grandma or Pete are the dreams. Dad's spaceman stories are more toilet than dream. Some of them are so bad you have to laugh. Once, he said Spaceman Toad was in trouble again, even though he had a monkey named George helping him pilot the ship. (My idea.) The ship got caught in the Milky Way. Stay in the milk too long and your engine gets gooey. Spaceman Toad radioed Spaceman Sam Winkie and said, Don't be a grumpy bumpy. Use your special powers to get me out. Sam Winkie said he needed Spacegirl Puss's help. But she had stopped playing with her younger friends. She thought she was sophisticated; she thought she was grown-up. If you don't get me out of the Milky Way quick, said Toad, I'll wind up a sour toad. At least you won't be a sourpuss, said Spaceman Sam Winkie, who ought to know. (I interrupted him: Dad, I said, I'd *never* say something that goofy.) In the end Spaceman Sam Winkie and Spacegirl Puss drove their ships around and around until a corner of the Milky Way turned into a bubbly shake, and they radioed Toad to drive his ship straight at the skin of the bubble, and it burst and, ta-da, out he flew. (*What?* said Mom in her I-don't-want-the-kids-to-hear voice. *You* try making these things up, answered Dad.) They got the milkshake idea from a famous astronaut who was friends with George the monkey and who once took a bath in our house. I remember Dad talking about an astronaut who smashed his skull in our bathtub, but I can't remember the rest of the story. At the motel, called the COLONIAL on the sign—Is it named after my grandpa? I asked, because Dad told me I was the grandson of Colonel Charlie Foran—Grandma surprised Mom by offering to give me a bath. I stepped into the water without testing it. My foot turned tomato and I cried. Oh Ruthie, said Mom, slapping a cold washcloth on my feet. Don't your children like hot baths? asked Grandma. The best thing about taking baths is sinking your body under the surface. The time I nearly drowned in a pool—I was three, I think—what I loved best was being swallowed up. I felt like a baby in his mom's arms; I felt like a kid in a rocking chair. In water or, better, under water, you feel held and secure. You know where you are, where you should be. When they pulled me out of the pool and asked if I was okay, I wished I hadn't been too young—and too busy puking, probably—to answer. I wished I'd said this: I'm okay but I'm breathing again, and that is sad. Don't know why, but it is.

God in heven

Us on erth

Fish in the see

What are you writing? asks Puss.

I erase the words with my sleeve.

Spaz, she says.

Stinky butt, adds Toad.

Say that again and I'll—

It's true, says Puss. You smell like—

Sing Ontary-ary-ary-oh, Toad, I interrupt.

He sings it.

I pull the collar way up and the cap way down. I sink into the mindshaft. I follow it

Down		Heven
into	or	into
Hell		up

or I stay near the middle, called Purgatory for Catholics and Limbo for babies who die before they're baptized. In Limbo babies float in milk for ever. In Purgatory Catholics wait for an invitation into heaven. Dead Catholics only: if you're alive, you're here on earth. We learned all this in Catechism with Father Ferguson. Before Grade Two started, I had the dumbest ideas about God. One time, after we visited Grandpa's farm, I told Mom that God was a wizard with silver hair and a pointy hat. Plus a cloak. Plus a wand. God lived on a cloud, I explained, where he sat all day smoking cigarettes and waving instructions to angels. Make me five horses, he would order. Make me ten cats, fifteen dogs and a hundred people. Puss was listening and she said it was probably a sin to say that God smokes. Mom, I remember, touched her arm and answered: He's just a boy, Debbie. He doesn't even know what that word means. (Toad was way worse. Mom asked him what God was, and he replied: God is a restaurant.) Now, of course, I know what a sin is and I know what God looks like: long white hair and a beard, angry blue eyes and snake-veins in his neck. Father Ferguson showed us a picture and taught us the rules and regulations of Catholicness. He taught us about obeying the Ten Commandments and recepting the Seven Sacraments: Baptism and Penance, Communion and Confirmation, Holy Orders and Marriage, plus a weird one for when you die. (Don't forget Masturbation, said Lenny Grusa, making some boys giggle.) He taught us about sins, which are stains on our souls. There are two types: venial and mortal. Venial sins are bad, but you get forgiven at confession; mortal sins send you straight to hell, no return ticket. As well, our souls are smeared with a sin we're born with, called original. Blame Adam and Eve for that one. A snake convinced them to steal an apple. He was the devil and was hoping to land them in trouble. It worked: Adam and Eve got kicked out of the Garden of Eden, an amazing place with waterfalls and trees of forbidding fruit. After Eden they tried the earth. There, they had kids who had kids who had kids who had us. I have freckles because my dad does. I have original sin because of Adam and Eve. The devil has pointy horns and a sharp tail and crispy-chicken skin. He makes people do terrible things. He's in charge of hell. But Father Ferguson didn't only want to talk about the bad stuff. He also wanted to tell us children about God. The one true God. The creator of heaven and earth. Who loves us all. In whose eyes we— as Catholic boys and girls—are special. God watches over his flock. He judges if we are co-operating in divine grace.

(Also if we are naughty or nice.) Jesus Christ was his only son. First he was the Christ child. Then he was an adult who got crucified. Tied to a cross: nails in his hands and feet, a crown of thorns on his head. *Forgive them, Father*, said Jesus to his dad, *they know not what they do.* He's bleeding and dying on the cross in the church and on the crucifix in every class in the school and also on a tiny cross beside the light switch in Mom and Dad's bedroom. (In Blind River Christ is crucified in most rooms in most houses my aunts and uncles live in. When he's not hanging on the cross, he's in a picture with his chest split open and his heart the same purple-pink colour that Jimmy Reilly turns when he's embarrassed. Sometimes Jesus' mom, the Virgin Mary, is next to him. Her chest is also purple-pink.) Father Ferguson said that Christ died for our sins, which tied the Catechism lessons up nicely: in the beginning was sin and in the end was sin too. A lot of the stuff the priest talked about was new, but some of it I remembered from my last trip to Blind River. Debbie and a girl cousin called Ginette told me about the babies in limbo. They cried talking about them. Cried and cried: the poor innocent babies. I felt sad about the babies and also angry—What did they do to deserve limbo? They were hardly born!—but I didn't cry. Then Luc said he'd show me where the devil lived. He and I walked back to the mindshaft behind town. Luc stepped right to the rim again. You down there, devil? he shouted into the hole. Come look, he told me. But I was having trouble moving. I'd just realized an amazing thing: Luc and *tante* Marie and *oncle* Rény and just about everyone else in Blind River spoke a different English than I did. Different words. (Gross becks!) Different sounds in their mouths. Was this an accent? Also, my legs were trembling. I wound up crawling on my hands and knees. Near the rim I poked my head over. Air shot up from the darkness. Cold air, not what I was expecting. Tell the devil to go fuck hisself, said Luc. Are you sure hell is down there? I asked him. Damn sure, he said. Kids falls in, they never come back, eh? They're in hell. Trapped down there with—

Hiccup!

Someone frighten Charlie, says Dad. It's the only way to make them stop.

Does Mom have an accent as well? She must, though I've never heard it. I am about to ask her when everything goes crazy. I get thrown against the door; Puss rolls off the window sill; Toad flies into the front seat. Dad swears and hunches over the wheel.

If you see a gas station . . . , says Mom.

I'll gladly pull in, he answers, his voice hard. For now, though, we keep moving. We don't have a choice.

Pete didn't have a choice, either. The day before Grade Two started, he told me another knock-knock joke. The FOR SALE sign on his lawn was now a SOLD. A truck sat in his driveway. Knock knock, said Pete. Who's there? I answered. Pete is home, he said. Pete is home who? Pete is home today but gone tomorrow! He smiled, so I smiled back, but I didn't think it was funny. His family moving away was just the weirdest thing to happen that summer. One day Pete and I were in our usual spot in the ditch, saying *hellur* and *och* to Graham Nester, who answered, *Gud day to ye bairns* and laughed when I asked if Robert-the-Bruce, also known as Robbie, barked with a Scottish accent, and the next—okay, two weeks later when we returned from up north—the ditch was filled in. Men riding on rolling pins were smoothing the earth where we'd sat. Others were spreading jamrolls of new grass. The ditches were gone and the road had been repaved and now we had curbs. Good for ball hockey, said Pete. But the ditch, I replied. Our special place . . . My new street doesn't even have ditches, he said. That's for old neighbourhoods. The day after my birthday, steamshovels started to chew up the fields at Longmore. Dad said they were going to build townhouses there. Within a week, machines also went to work on the Bumpity. (Run for your life, Box Man! Pete and I shouted.) Mom said it was like being in a noise sandwich. You can't think for the clamour, said Graham Nester. (It sounded like this: *Ye cannae think fur de chlamor.*) Then, to top it all, the moving van backed out of the Nicolsons' driveway. His mom and dad crossed to say goodbye. George walked over and stood beside me, as if we were now best friends. Allan stopped his bicycle. So long, he said to Pete and—I couldn't believe this—Pete answered, See you, Allan. As if they were buddies! As if he knew all about Allan and his haunted house! Knock knock, said Pete to George. Who's there? answered George. What, said Pete to him (but smiling at me), you don't remember who I am?

Not funny, I say out loud.

You must be hot inside your jacket, says Mom.

Don't you get it? says Puss. He stinks!

Debbie . . ., answers Mom.

Somebody does, agrees Dad. It smells like Old Spice. I didn't think I put on *that* much this morning.

My sister looks at me.

Please, I ask her without speaking.

Who can tell me what the capital of Manitoba is? says Dad.

Groan, replies Debbie.

Phew, says Mom. This sure is a long ride.

Trailer for sale or rent, sings Dad. He drums his fingers on the wheel. *Rooms to let, fifty cents / No phone, no pool, no pets / I ain't got no—*

Use your special powers, says Toad to me.

I haven't any, Toad, I would answer, if I wanted to talk. I'm a kid trapped in a freezer. I'm a baby in limbo. (*Don't just sit there, Mom. Don't just stare out the window at the storm, brow crinkled, teeth biting lips. Look at ME! Help ME!*) If Puss wasn't watching I'd take my glove off and write four letters on the window. I'd write them big and not erase them. The letters are in English but the word, or maybe the words, they spell are in another language. I can't even pronounce them normally: *IN-RI* I guess, like Henry. I stare at these letters at mass or in the classroom or even beside the light switch in our house. (KING OF THE JEWS, they spell. But wasn't Jesus a Catholic? asked John Sealy in Catechism. He was the *first* Catholic, answered Father Ferguson. Only, because of where he grew up, he happened to be raised a Jew.) When Missus Gordon got angry with me for holding my pencil between the wrong fingers—Look at everyone else in class, she said. Don't you want to write the way they do?—I glanced at the letters at his feet and thought, Okay, I'll try. Missus Gordon told me later that she wasn't angry at all. She only wanted to correct a problem. You're one of two southpaws this year, she said. You both need extra work. My place in the class makes it easy to get help. As soon as I saw the globe screwed into the counter at the front, I asked for the first desk in the window row. Kids who say I was a suck to choose that spot must not notice how I spin the globe every chance I get, staring at the continents and countries, feeling the mountains under my fingertips. Even when I'm seated I still look at it, especially the blue parts that Dad says are the seven seas. I love thinking about seas and oceans. I love thinking about the world as a globe spinning through space. Missus Gordon says I'm a good little thinker. My report card agreed last week. Even though I can read now, I asked Mom to read the tiny print on the back. *The purpose of education is to mould and fashion "the true and finished man of character,"* said the report card. *It should begin in the home and be continued in the school. Parents, teachers and children must co-operate in this high and holy task.* Understand? she asked. Kind of, I lied. There was more: *To these natural virtues necessary for honourable manhood and worthy citizenship, the Catholic teacher will impart a supernatural motive based on the example and love of the Christ child. Religious teachings and practice will crown and unite all our teaching and character formation. Thus the natural virtues will be elevated to the supernatural order . . .* What's super— I began to ask. I'm not sure, answered Mom, frowning the same way she does when she reads about *mackintoshes* and *larders*. Blah blah blah, said Dad, sipping his coffee. Let me finish, Dave, said Mom. *Catholic parents and teachers, by giving the child a love for prayer and by promoting union with Christ through participation in the Mass and the reception of the Sacraments, will co-operate with divine grace in forming the true and perfect Christian.* Signed, Philip F. Pocock, coad—coadjutor Archbiship of Toronto. Phew, she added. You mean Missus Gordon didn't write my report card? I asked. Sure she did, answered Mom. Those were general words for all students. Here is what Missus Gordon said about you. *Charles is a very good student whose work is*— Get to the thinking part, I interrupted. Okay, she said. Let's see . . . *Although Charles' work is done very well and is very neat, he becomes discouraged if he comes upon a*— That's not about thinking, I said again. Don't be impatient, replied Mom. Hurry up, Moo, said Dad. It's past his bedtime. Can I try your coffee? I asked Dad. You won't like it, he answered. I sipped from the mug. He was right: it tasted awful. Mmm, I said. I like it! Where was I . . . , said Mom. Oh yes—*if he comes upon a problem he cannot grasp at a glance, or if he makes an error. We should impress upon Charles that sometimes there are*— M-O-M, I said. M-O-O, said Dad. She looked at us both. Fine, she said. I won't even finish if you don't— It's past my bedtime, I explained to her. Attaboy, said Dad, ruffling my hair. Mom sighed. Here it is . . . *sometimes there are problems that are not so easily solved. Therefore we must ask for advice or slowly think the problem out.* She stopped. *Slowly think the problem out,* she repeated. See, you're a good thinker. Have a good night, thinker, said Dad. I'll think about it, I replied. A joke, he said. From a seven–year-old! But in bed, face washed and pyjamas on, I didn't have a chance to think. I had to pray instead. Mom knelt beside me. NOW I LAY— Softly, she said, glancing over at Toad in the other bed. You can whisper. God hears everything. Is he in the room? I asked. He's everywhere, she answered. Is he talking to my guardian angel? Maybe, she said. Now pray. Toad mumbled from inside a dream. *Now I lay me down to sleep,* I said, waiting for Mom to join in. *I pray the Lord my soul to keep. If I should*— I stopped. Why would I die before I wake? I wondered. You won't, she said. But say it anyway. *If I should die before I wake, I pray the Lord my soul to take.* Good, she said. Now let's do the Our Father. If I died tonight, I asked, where would God take my soul? Up to heaven, she replied. But you're a child. You're not going to— Would my guardian angel let him? I interrupted. After all, she's here to protect me. He's God, Charlie, replied Mom. Not a robber! He wants my soul, doesn't he? I said. What if I don't want to—? Shh, she said. Too late: Toad mumbled again and, still half in a dream, spoke some words. At first I thought he said *geddygeddyoh.* Then I listened again: *Ontaryaryaryoh,* said my baby brother. Do souls have wings? I whispered to Mom. Enough for tonight, she answered, standing up. But you wanted me to think! I complained. And this is hard stuff for a kid to figure out. Think inside your head, she said. God will hear you. I crawled into bed. God probably has millions of kids trying to speak with him right now, I told her. I think I'll talk to my guardian angel instead. She's right there—I pointed to a spot beyond my feet—and is probably bored. Good idea, replied Mom. She shut the door and I pulled the blankets up to my chin. For the first time in ages I missed having Leo and Sylvester with me. (Mom is keeping them in a closet, in case I change my mind.) They'd enjoy a chat with an angel. There she was too, floating above my feet. White wings and a white dress, a halo on her head and a wand in her hand. Her hair golden. Her eyelashes fluttery. Poor angel, I said to her. Stuck here with us. I'm sure you'd rather be home in heaven. I'm sure that's your proper place. In

	Heven	
above	Purgitory	Limbo (on the side, I guess)
above	Hell	

What about Eden? I wonder. What about the earth? Where do they go on the map? Where is their—?

That's not how you spell heaven, says Puss.

What?

It has an A in it. Let me—

She reaches across. I beat her to the window and, pinching my jacket cuff in my fingers, wipe the words off. All of them: *swoosh.*

I was just trying to teach you something, says my sister.

Now, children, says Mom.

We're almost at the big highway, offers Dad. The drive will be easier then. It may even be starting to clear.

We're *never* going to get out of here, says Puss. And Charlie's smell is making me sick.

You stinky, adds Toad.

Mom swivels around in her seat. Did you open the Old Spice that Grandma Ruthie gave you?

She said I was a big boy, I reply. She said young gentlemen should smell nice.

How much did you use?

Half the bottle, says Puss.

A real little Frenchman, agrees Dad.

Pépé-le-Pew, says Puss.

Toad holds his nose.

Dumb, I say to myself.

This time I unzip the jacket and, the hat still on, pull it over my head. Then I zip the jacket back up. Light turns to dark. Dark turns to black. The air boils and the Old Spice reeks, but at last I'm alone. Am I a little Frenchman? Mom is. My aunts and uncles are also, though they sure don't stink like this. Grandma Ruthie isn't French and she wears buckets of perfume and gives kisses that remind me of Christmas cake. The cologne was her gift. We opened our presents at the motel, even though Christmas wasn't for three weeks. She said she had a special gift for Charlie, and later on Mom explained that Grandma was making up for accidentally calling me Ricky, who is my cousin. That happened the day before. When I answered, But I'm Charlie Foran: Don't you know who I am? Grandma got upset. Of course I know who Charlie Foran is, she said. I've known about him since long before *you* were born, child. I didn't understand but then I made it worse, I guess, by asking her again if the motel was named after Grandpa. Mom put her hands on my shoulders and told me to go watch TV with Toad. I didn't see Grandma for the rest of the day. When we opened gifts the next morning, though, I was given two packages, which made Puss sulk and Toad cry. Mom took us aside and said that the cologne was a special gift from Grandma, because of what happened. (What happened? asked Puss. Beats me, I answered.) I could probably think about Grandma Ruthie enough to figure it out, but I'd rather not. The Old Spice, which looks like water, is a taste in my mouth. The host at mass, which is the body of Jesus Christ, has no taste. When Father Ferguson said that first communion meant eating God's son, a lot of us were disgusted. He said that communion was a mystery—the mystery of the covenant—and that by taking the Eucharist we gave thanks to the Lord. Father didn't expect us to understand it. But he reminded the class that Jesus also said he was the bread of life, and he who eats that bread will live forever. Then Lenny Grusa asked if toasting the bread of life made any difference and the priest shook his jowls. Lenny returned from the office with pink hands. He raised his palms to show us the ruler whacks. Father Ferguson went nuts at that: screaming and pulling his ear, even though I'm sure Lenny wasn't thinking of the crucifix. (I thought of it right away.) He was sent back to the office again. Sister Mary Wyatt, also red and jowly, paid us a visit to tell the story of the children who fell from grace with God and wound up regretting their sins very much. Lenny stood beside her, the tears waterfalling off his nose. At recess kids still made jokes about Catholic vampires and at lunch the next day, when I asked Jimmy about his sandwich, he answered: I've got Jesus, with cheese and mustard. I had baloney, which kind of looked like . . . Well, I nearly barfed. From now on, I told Mom that afternoon, peanut butter sandwiches only. By the time first communion came, we were all ready to barf. Father Ferguson had also told us about the part of mass where the priest goes over to a small altar, opens a box and takes out the consecrated body of Jesus Christ. Both Grade Two classes sat in the front rows of the church watching Father get an extra large order of Jesus from the tabernacle. We were too nervous in our jackets and ties and dresses—also with our parents and grandparents and, for some kids, aunts and uncles and cousins behind us—to make jokes. Kids said that if you dropped the host, you went to purgatory for a year. If you gagged on Christ or spit him out, the penalty was ten years. If you refused to eat Jesus, of course, you went to hell for eternity. (A long, long time.) Grade Five altar boys rang the bells and we shuffled up with our hands in steeples and our heads bowed. Father Ferguson started at the far end, a boy angel holding a gold plate under each chin. THE BODY OF CHRIST, said Father. One, two, three children said AMEN and stuck out their tongues. I was seventh. THE BODY OF CHRIST, he said. AMEN, answered John Sealy next to me. Father Ferguson stepped sideways. He glanced at my face and then looked down into his cup for an ordinary-sized piece. (Lenny,

who sins the most in Grade Two, probably got an entire toe.)
THE BODY OF CHRIST, said the priest. I stuck my tongue
out. I also closed my eyes. Everyone said you couldn't watch.
But how could I be sure the host landed safely? I opened
them back up fast and looked down, trying to find my
mouth below my nose. That made me dizzy. That made
me—

Boo!

Aaah! I say, driving my head into the top of the jacket.
The zipper stays zipped but I hear a rip. Sweat stings my
eyes. My stomach somersaults. Not a chance I'll come out
now, though. Not after what Puss—

See, she says. He's stopped hiccupping.

Hiccup, I say.

That's fake.

HICCUP, I repeat, faking it.

I also forgot to say amen *before* Father Ferguson gave me
the host. Once it's on your tongue, talking may shoot it
back out. I guess my eyes showed how terrified I was,
because Father snorted and said, Amen, I'm sure, and
moved on. I made the secret Catholic sign. In the pew, I
could see other kids working to scrape Jesus Christ down
from the roofs of their mouths. I knelt there, waiting for
him to melt—*Never* chew the host, said Father: Let it dis-
solve—thinking how the Eucharist didn't taste like sausage
or baloney. It didn't taste like anything. It just was. At the
end of mass I made the secret sign again. Even though I'd
been doing it since Mom started taking me to church years
ago, I practised for weeks in the bathroom. I loved the fast

and easy way adults made the sign. I wanted to do it the same.

Now, I try making the sign inside the jacket. Too tight. Too hot. So I unzip—the cold air slaps my face—and write in the Name of the—

	Father	
Spirit	AMEN	and the Holy
	and the Son	

I know what that is, says Puss.

For once, I don't erase the words.

You're soaked in sweat, says Mom. She reaches over the seat for my forehead. She wants to rub it, I can tell, but it's too far and her arm gets tired. I lean forward so she can at least feel my skin and bone.

Use your special powers, Pépé-le-Pew, says Toad.

Don't go back inside, okay? asks Mom. I don't want you to disappear forever.

I'm melting, says Puss. I'm melting!

Okay, Mom, I answer. (*Thanks*, I add inside my head. *Thanks for rescuing me.*)

Will you look at that, says Dad, pointing out the front windshield. For a second I see only fluttering snow and murky light. Then I follow his directions beyond the car and the highway. High up in the sky, the dark clouds have split open and the split part is bright, light pouring down in a beam. I think of two things. First, of walking through drying sheets on the clothesline in the backyard. The fresh smell of the sheets: their soft touch against my face. Second,

I think of the light that slants into my room sometimes, which I used to sit in. If I could, I'd love to go stand in the shaft from heaven. If I could find where it hit the ground, and if I was allowed to step inside, I'd be happy to stay there. For eternity. For a long, long time.

Beautiful, says Mom.

We'll be home in an hour, says Dad.

Amen, I reply.

He made the sign of the cross again, says my sister.

I want to write words, announces Toad.

Here we go, sighs Dad.

Watch this, I tell my brother.

I rub the window clean. Then, thinking about the poor kids in fridges and freezers and imagining that they are riding the beam of light up to heaven, riding safe and innocent to God, I write the only four letters Toad needs to know:

I N R I

1968

Things to Do in April

1. Pull cookie eyes out of snowmen melting on lawns. Snap their carrot noses. Kick them over—*pow!*

2. Watch workmen finish the apartments up at Longmore. A sign says they're the Willowtree Estates. Watch workmen finish houses where the Bumpity used to be. Families are already moving in there. Allan-the-ghost-boy left sometime during the winter. Pete Nicolson moved away last summer. His new house has a staircase that turns as you climb it and a basement with a pool table. We play in the basement while our moms drink coffee. I want to be lots of fun, but it isn't. I want Pete to look the way he used to—the way I remember him, I guess—but he doesn't: his legs are too long and his smile is all wrong and even his voice is strange (he's missing his front teeth). He has more hair now. His ears don't seem so Dumbo. Kids are funny sometimes, aren't they? says Tom when I ask to leave early. Allan's house is still FOR SALE. No way anyone will move into it.

3. Think about the King who just died.

Charles Foran

What Jimmy Says About the Dead King

1. He was married to a queen. That made him a pope. Is the Pope dead? I ask Missus Grundel. Nonsense, child, she answers. He's doing just fine.

2. He was an American king. America is the United States or the States or even just the U-S. On the globe, it is a country below Canada with different-coloured provinces, called states, and some really big bumps, called the Rocky Mountains, that run down one side. In real life, America is all the cities and land across from Niagara Falls. Debbie says you have to swim to get there. Dad says you need a barrel. Mom says they're having trouble in the States, including their war in Vietnam. First, their war: now, their dead king. In America they make the best television: *The Bugs Bunny–Roadrunner Hour, Davy Crockett* and— *slam! pow!*—*Batman.* In Canada we make *The Friendly Giant* and *Romper Room* and a new show called *Mr. Dress-Up.* They are also good, though not fast or exciting, the way TV should be. Commander Tom, who runs Rocketship Seven, lives in Buffalo. Poor Commander Tom, says Dad.

3. The dead king was black. A black American king. I study the pictures in the classroom again. The Queen and the Pope aren't black. Nor is Jesus on the cross, though he has a tan. Grade Three hasn't any black kids. Grade Six has one boy, but I only see him in the schoolyard. At church two Sundays ago a black family sat in the pew in front of us. They were beautiful, especially their choco-

late cream eyes, but they also made me uncomfortable. Mom whispered that staring was rude.

Why Jesus Has a Tan

1. He lived in a country where the sun was hot all the time and it never snowed. So hot, a man got crucified in his underwear. So hot, you'd drink vinegar.
2. Varnish, says Dad.
3. I don't have a third reason.

Why I Like to Make Lists

1. Mom thinks it's weird talking this way.
2. It helps sort out the thousands of thoughts racing around in my head all at once, always, day and night, winter spring summer fall.
3. Lists are fast. Lists mean things happen quickly. Like instructions on the sides of games. Step one when you're almost eight years old: make lists. Step two: explain why your lists have only three things.

Why My Lists Have Only Three Things

1. Father, Son and the Holy Goat.
2. Heaven, Earth and Hell.
3. Grandpa, Dad and Me. (Also Toad, I guess.)

Three Lists I Wrote Out and Handed to Mom, to Be Put on the Refrigerator Door

#1 Foods I Really Hate

1. brussels sprouts (puke).
2. liver (double puke).
3. blood sausage (too pukey for words).

#2 Foods I Really Love

1. hamburger mush.
2. Mikes-in-the-hole (heh heh).
3. ordinary sausage.

#3 Why Mom Should Feed Me Foods I Like

1. I'll be her sweet boy all the time. Say my prayers. Do my homework. Play with my brother.
2. Good moms who feed their children only foods they like go to heaven. Okay moms, who feed their children peas and carrots and rice and brown bread, have to spend a few years in purgatory. Terrible moms, who fry liver and claim it will taste better with bacon on top, or who won't let their son leave the table until he eats at least one brussels sprout, go straight to he . . . he . . . Hamilton.
3. I'll promise not to put any more lists on the fridge.

Why I Don't Mind Playing With Toad Now That He Is Four

1. You say, Hey, Toad, I bet you can't pretend Josy-the-cat is a horse, and he answers, Yes, I can, and he sits on Josy and says, Ride 'em, cowboy! At first, the cat stands there looking confused. Then she collapses. If Toad says, Giddyap! and slaps Josy's bum, the cat goes *grrrr* and her eyes turn black. Toad, I say, she's going to scratch you. Better get off. He won't, though. He'll just repeat, Giddyap! and rock back and forth until— Scratch! Slash!

2. You have gas, I say to him. You have gas, he answers back. No, *you* have gas, Toad. Me have gas, he agrees. Right, Toad has gas. Right, he says, Toad has gas. Go tell Mom, I whisper. Go tell her she has gas. But don't say who told you.

   And you know what? He does. Toad has gas, Mom, he says. Do you? she answers. You have gas too, Mom, he adds. Do I? she replies. And who told you to say that?
   Heh heh.

3. Debbie is busy with Brownies and gymnastics and, besides, she isn't my older sister anymore—she's a girl. George is my best friend on the street now, except for Graham Nester, who is about a hundred years old, and Robert-the-Bruce, who is a pooch. George and I play in his basement. A boy named Keith Healy lives behind the Campbells and he comes over. He's good at making stuff. He orders us about. Jimmy Reilly is my bestest best friend. We've both joined the 7th Lansing cub troop and

begun to learn hockey: Blessed Trinity, Junior Tyke, though neither of us exactly made the team. Jimmy already has a sister and a brother and his mom just had another baby. He can't hang around the schoolyard or watch TV at my house every afternoon. That leaves Toad. He's always there. He always says yes. (He just wants to be with you, says Mom. Please try to remember that.) Want to play ball, Charlie? he asks. Want to go fish?

Why Jimmy and I Were Both Made Goalies

1. We couldn't stand up on the ice.
2. Goalies can hold onto those red bars. Coach Byrne told Jimmy and me to stay in the middle of the net, but we couldn't reach the bars from there. Dad said I should just lie across the ice, since none of the kids can lift the puck yet.
3. We had to pick Jimmy up, and arrived late to the first team practice. The coach said the last two boys to appear had to play goal.

What Happened the Only Time I Played

1. Coach Byrne let us each play a practice game, to see if we wanted to return in the fall. I went first. It snowed the whole game. The wind smacked my face. My hands

turned pink and my ears burned. I asked Dad for a hat. With the hat on, the eyeholes in my mask were too high. I tried to squish the helmet, but the puck went in. I tried to look out the nose holes, but the puck went in. I even tried to sit on my bum and stare into the snow, but the puck still went in. Twenty-eight times. Twenty-eight goals. Our side lost.

2. Jimmy let in twenty-four goals during his game. He said that meant he was a better goalie. It meant he was going to play in the NHL. The day he played it wasn't snowing or windy or even that cold. His hands didn't turn pink and his nose didn't run and he didn't need a hat.

3. The coach said he'd see us boys in October, unless we'd learned our lesson. And for God's sake, Dave, he added, make sure they play lots of road hockey!

Who I Play Road Hockey With

1. Bobby Avery, who takes slush slapshots, the two Warden boys, Jimmy and George, who doesn't like hockey but wants to be with us, plus Toad, who has no idea what's going on so we make him referee. I wear my pads and gloves and mask, even though Bobby is the only one who can shoot the ball hard, and even though the only time he really hurts me—Bobby Hull shoots, he scores! he shouts—the equipment is no help. The tennis ball smashes my penis. For a second I think it just stings. Then I'm sure I'm going to puke. Jimmy and Bobby help

me up. Got you where you lived, eh? says Bobby. In the bathroom, I pull down my pants. The penis looks okay, but the sack underneath it is gone. Knocked up into my stomach. Knocked down into my socks.

2. Kids from over on Dunforest. Keith Healy is one of them, and he challenges us to a game. I want to say no, but I can't think of a reason. Also Bobby's look says: *Don't be a suck.* Right away, Jimmy gets whacked on the knuckles and a boy trips George. Bobby punches a kid who must be ten and another one raises his stick to Jimmy and says: You'll pay for that, asshole. Graham Nester comes along with Robbie. He walks into the middle of the game. *Doan't furse me to let the animal luuse,* he warns. *He'll tur the hide off ye rascals.* Robbie is a sausage with fur over his eyes and a bark like a toy that George got for Christmas. I'm surprised when the boys from Dunforest quit. Come on, says Keith Healy. These guys stink. Next day, while I'm playing catch with Toad, Graham stops to chat. It's windy out, though, so all I hear is: *Arrgh occht arrgh occht, laddie.*

3. Allan-the-ghost-boy. He just shows up one afternoon and asks if he can play. I say sure and George says sure, but both of us are surprised. He is taller than I am now and has on a windbreaker and torn running shoes. I know for sure it's Allan when he begins to chew the fingers of his glove. (He used to bite his nails too.) He looks at Pete's house and says: How's Pete? Afterwards, he walks back up the block to his old place. His stick drags on the pavement. He nearly slips on a patch of ice.

Things That Make Me Feel Weird in April

1. Hearing a word at school and then, half knowing it is bad, still asking Mom what it means. Don't ever say that again, she answers. If you do, I'll wash your mouth out with soap. Okay, okay, I promise, leaving the kitchen fast. Alone in my room, I say it anyway: CUNT. Then I spell it on the window: C U N T. The word doesn't look awful. Sounds mean, though.

2. Missus Grundel catching me picking my nose. I am at the back of the row, where no one can see me, and though I usually use a tissue, honest, or raise my hand for the bathroom, honest, it's *really* itchy up there. All she does is stare at me. Stare and frown, her expression saying: *I'm disappointed in you.* I bet my face is red. I know I have to hold back tears.

3. The way kids treat Nellie Parker. Parker the pig, they call her, Parker the pig. With a face like an ass and an ass twice as big! She's got the cooties. Touch her, you catch them too; touch someone else, you pass them on. In the yard, a Grade Four boy calls her a cunt.

Why British Bulldog Is More Fun in May

1. The ground isn't as wet. Your clothes get dirty, but not destroyed. Destroy your clothes and Missus Grundel sends you to the locker room for your shorts. You look like a dork. Worse, Sister Mary Wyatt might notice you

in the hallway and ask, What were you doing at lunch to get so dirty? If you answer, Milk carton hockey, she won't believe you fell that often. If you answer, Skipping, she'll just laugh. If you answer, British Bulldog, the principal will say, Aha, and tell you that she appreciates your honesty. Then she'll order a man teacher to strap you three times on each hand. (No more ruler: it's a real strap now.) Don't say you didn't know, Sister Mary will add before the man—usually the Grade Seven teacher, Mister Harkness—pulls you into the space between the front door and the entranceway or down into the gym. Don't say you hadn't been warned.

2. BRITISH BULLDOG IS A VIOLENT GAME, said the announcement back in April. IT IS STRICTLY FORBIDDEN. ANYONE CAUGHT PLAYING IT IN THE SCHOOLYARD WILL BE . . .

3. It is pretty rough. You line up at the edge of the pavement. One boy is It to start. (Girls can't play.) The It kid says, One, two, three—go! and everyone races for the back fence. The boy tackles a runner, usually the fattest, and then those two gang up on someone else. On and on it goes, until there is only a single kid left. He's the winner. He also gets to choose the new It. Last year, boys from Grade Two all the way to Grade Seven played together. I didn't, but Lenny Grusa and Lucci Pavese and a few others tried. Their hair got pulled and their clothes got torn and they wore mud masks with blood mixed in. Except for Lenny, they wound up crying. Except for Lenny, you could tell they were scared. Sister Mary

Wyatt was certain someone would end up at the hospital. She was positive a bone would break. That's why she started to get tough about British Bulldog. That's why teachers on yard duty started to wander out to the field, instead of standing near the doors smoking cigarettes and talking to suck-ups. This year someone decided to divide the games: Grades Two to Five, Grades Six to Eight. Now I'm not the youngest and I'm not fat and I'm an okay size for my age. Being tackled hurts, of course, but playing is fast and fun and I get to run, run, run.

Why It's Great When Mom Goes to Blind River for a Few Days and Dad Looks After Us

1. We get to eat in restaurants. Come on, kids, he says when he gets home from work and our babysitter, who is called Sue and isn't all there, leaves: Let's go get some fish and chips. (And it's not even Friday!) We eat fish and chips or hamburger steaks and then we help Dad put up signs for Trudeaumania. Debbie reads addresses from a list. Dad stops the car outside a house. Toad and I take a red-and-white sign from the trunk and drag it onto the lawn. Dad whacks the sign with a hammer until it stands up and a man named Pierre Elliott Trudeau smiles at us on both sides of the cardboard. He wears a suit and tie. He's our choice for Pope.

   Prime minister, says Dad with a laugh.

2. We make our own lunches. No baloney. No sandwich, actually, or fruit. Four cookies, two sugar doughnuts,

plus some chocolate kisses I found in the secret candy drawer in the buffet. (They fell out, I usually have to say. I picked them up off the floor!) I feel fine after lunch. Missus Grundel doesn't need to send me to the nurse. The nurse doesn't need to make me lie on the couch until the colour returns to my face.

3. No baths.

Why It's Weird When Mom Goes Away

1. When Dad is away on business, I climb onto the toilet bowl and open the cabinet above the sink. On his shelf are combs in a glass, a brush in a mug, a razor with a gold handle, a jar of hair gel, plus two bottles of Old Spice. (I'm waiting until I'm older to use mine.) When Dad is away, I wrap one of his ties around my neck and find a pipe. Any coffee, Moo? I ask Mom, clomping around the kitchen in his shoes. That fella is as dumb as a sack of hammers! I say as well.

When Mom goes to Blind River for a few days to visit her sisters, I don't do much, except maybe slip into their bedroom. I never touch the brushes and mirrors on her dresser. I never open her closet. When Mom is away, I get quiet. When she calls at supper, I'm first to the phone. I love you, she says. I love you too, I answer, not caring if Debbie makes a face or Toad says yuck. (They both say they love her as well.) *Des gros becs,* she adds. Gross becs back to you, Mom, I reply. The sound of her voice makes me excited and warm and sad. I even hum a song I used to sing with her. I can't remember the words, but the song comes into my head. *La-la-la-la-la-la,* I hum. *La-la-la-la.* Then I go look at her photo in the living room. Dad is in the picture too, but I ignore him. The photo was taken before us kids were born. Mom isn't Mom in it; she is a girl named Muriel married to a boy named Dave. Living in a house and eating meals and going for walks without the children who are the joys of their life. If Debbie, me and Toad weren't born then, where were we? Father Ferguson and Father Arnot have never talked about where kids live before they grow inside their mom's tummy and come out her private parts. I don't think I remember anything from that long ago. Where was I then? Where was the lonely boy?

2. I forget to say my prayers. At night I climb into bed and shut off the lamp. God will be disappointed if you forget, says Mom before she leaves. I won't forget, I answer, but then I do. Dad is no help. He just says, Sleep tight, Sam Winkie, and kisses me on the forehead. (His cheeks are bristly by bedtime. Tiny hairs have been growing all day! He also has a scent—his own special one—that makes me think of oranges with freckles.) Once, Mom was away for a Sunday and she made Dad promise to take us to mass. We went to a restaurant instead and ate bacon and eggs. When Mom got back, she said: Why didn't either of you remind your father about church? I forgot, lied Debbie. Me too, I lied as well. Only Toad told the truth: Restaurant is more fun! he said.

3. After school Debbie and I are babysat by Sue. (Toad is with her all day.) She smiles and laughs and says we're beautiful kids, just beautiful. She lets us eat doughnuts and cookies for snack, and watch all of *Rocketship Seven* and then barely touch our dinners, even though she tells Dad we cleaned our plates; and she's gentle and sweet, kind and nice, and wouldn't harm a fly or say boo to a goose. Still, I feel strange around her. Mom says she's *special*. Bobby Avery calls her a *retar*— Don't let me ever hear you use that word, commands Mom, reaching for the bar of soap. Understand? I don't exactly, but I answer, Yes, Mom, and race out of the kitchen (again). At the door I add: I wish I'd known that words could get you into so much trouble. Maybe I wouldn't have wanted to learn to read and write so badly!

Stuff That Is Wrong to Think and Do

1. Call anyone a retard. (Ooops.)
2. Make fun of Nellie Parker. Parker the pig! Nellie cooties! Kids say awful things about Nellie when she isn't in school and repeat them, pointing fingers and giggling, when she's at her desk, purple lips moving, eyes filling with water. (I have a cousin in Blind River named Elizabeth. Her lips are also purple. Her eyes are as big as a cow's.) Missus Grundel is ashamed, truly ashamed, at how the class treats Nellie Parker, and twice now she has escorted her down to the office to call her parents, daring

us to make a peep while she is gone. Make even a peep
. . . , she has warned. Nellie doesn't come back to class
those days and our teacher is in a bad mood until the
bell rings. Shame on you, she says as we put on our coats.
Shame on us all.

What's a torturer? I ask Mom after school one day. A
what? she says. Missus Grundel says that on certain days
we're no better than a pack of torturers. She wants me to
explain. Kids make fun of Nellie Parker because she
misses so much school, I begin. Also because she's fat
and has pale skin and doesn't wash her hair and some
kids say she smells. Do *you* say any of these terrible
things? asks Mom. Never, I answer. Do you try stopping
other children, especially in front of the girl? No, I
answer, my voice smaller. But I wish they wouldn't.

3. Sing this song: *Daniel Boone was a man / He was a big
man / But the bear was bigger / So he ran like a nigger / Up
a tree.* Nigger is another bad word. It means negro, also
called black. Chink is bad as well. (See what I mean
about words?) Mister Woo is a Chinese person, not a
Chink or a slanty-eyes. (*Me Chinaman / Me have fun /
Make lots of babies / Out my bum.*) I was wrong to call
Mister Woo those names, even behind his back. I was
wrong and I am sorry. Who am I saying sorry to? I
make the mistake of asking. Mister Woo, answers Mom.
But he can't hear me from our house, I say. Well, *I* can
hear you, she replies, and it's kind of the same thing.
Sorry, Mister Woo, I repeat to Mom, which is pretty stupid, though I sure don't say so.

Charles Foran

Interesting Things at Mister Woo's

1. I get my allowance on Saturday morning. Twenty cents,
    cash. Thanks, Dad, I say, and then I run to meet Jimmy
    out on Willowdale Avenue. We show each other our
    money. Sometimes he has only three nickels or a dime;
    his dad works at night, and you can't wake him up
    before lunch. Twenty cents buys two packs of hockey
    cards. Each pack has five cards plus a stick of gum. At
    least one of the five cards will make other boys want to
    do a trade: a Bruce Gamble for a Rogie Vachon, a Bobby
    Orr for three Maple Leafs *and* a Pocket Rocket Richard.
    Twenty cents also buys Popeye cigarettes and a Lola, ten
    blackballs and a Pez, tons of spaghetti licorice. Twenty
    cents buys a Cherry Blossom. Twenty cents buys an ice
    cream sandwich.

    We sit on the steps of Woo's grocery and compare bags.
    Dogs sniff us and cats curl around our legs. Kids throw
    bikes onto the sidewalk and storm inside. Cars stop and
    grown-ups buying milk and a newspaper say, Morning,
    boys. We sit and watch this; it's Saturday; we've got
    nothing to do. Mom makes me promise not to eat all my
    candy at once. At least wait until after lunch, she says.

2. Mister Woo has yellow-brown skin and almond eyes and
    hair so black it could be painted. When he glances down
    at you from behind the counter, his eyeballs float up over
    his glasses. His tummy is bigger than Dad's, but his arms
    aren't as hairy. He doesn't say much—Twenty cent, okay?
    No touch that, okay? Tell you mom no eggs today,

okay?—and he never smiles, probably because his teeth are crooked. Also, when he catches kids stealing stuff, he pinches them on the spot where the shoulder joins the neck. Then he calls their house. The pinch hurts—Jimmy and I tried it on each other—but having your dad drive up to the curb, slam the car door and step into the shop to get you probably hurts more. (Bobby Avery got spanked *and* grounded.) Missus Woo is nicer, a scarf tied in her hair and black slippers on her feet, and they have children who play in the yard. The oldest boy is about our age.

They live upstairs, you know, says Jimmy one Saturday, pointing to some windows over the store. Who does? I ask. Mister Woo and Missus Woo and their kids. No way, I say. Yes way, says Jimmy. You just don't understand, do you? Understand what? I have to ask. His answer makes me feel strange, though I can't explain why. Immigrants, he says.

I suck on a blackball, pretending I know what that word means. Is my tongue black yet? I ask him. Yup, he answers. We keep quiet for a while. Jimmy eats a cigarette. The Woos are Chinks, he suddenly says. I'm not. I'm Irish.

3. Just because I come home from the store with extra candy doesn't mean I stole it. Mom makes me empty the bag and then my pockets. Am I telling her that Mister Woo let me have two packs of cards, an Oh Henry! bar, a Sweet-Tart, five blackballs and some spaghetti licorice all for twenty cents? Honest, I answer. Honest? says Mom. Why you . . . She drags me to the car. Where are

we going? I ask, already sobbing. She parks outside Woo's and says, We'll see what you bought this morning. Don't, Mom, I beg. He tortures kids who . . . Kids who what? she asks.

Hello, Mister Woo, she says. Morning, he answers. Do you remember my son coming in earlier with his friend? asks Mom. Freckle boys, answers Mister Woo, almost smiling. She shows him the candy bag. And could Charlie have bought this candy for twenty cents? He takes the bag and asks, Twenty cent? First he glances down into it, his eyes still behind his glasses, and then he looks at me, the eyeballs popping up. He drops the bag on the counter. I bet he remembers me counting out forty-six cents and handing it to him. I bet he remembers Jimmy whispering how lucky I was that my dad hangs his pants in the bathroom. (His dad keeps his in a closet.) I bet Mister Woo remembers what happened. Kids steal, he finally says. No respect for anyone.

Mom makes me apologize. She also tries to pay the extra money. No money, he says twice, and then: Go home, talk to your boy.

I have to stay in my room until dinner. Dad comes in and says he hopes I've learned my lesson. I wipe the sawdust off his shirt and answer, For sure, Dad. Toad whispers through the door that I'm a bad boy. He also tells me he wants to be an animal doctor when he grows up. Debbie slips two pieces of Juicy Fruit gum under the wood, making me promise not to tell. All afternoon I wait for her. Listening for her footsteps. Hoping she'll be humming a happy French song. When she finally appears, her face is so sad I decide to cheer her up. Want some candy, Mom? I ask.

Why I'm a Bad Kid

1. I stole money from my dad.
2. At mass on Sunday, one hand on the railing and the other in my pocket, I look up at Jesus hanging on the cross and wonder if he has a penis. Underneath his cloth: where men and boys from cold countries put zippers. All men and boys have penises, I'm pretty sure: none of them have chinas or vaginas or cu– –s. You have to have one thing or the other. You have to choose. Kids in Grade One and Two call them dicks and weenies, but kids in Grade Four use the word COCK. Guys stick their COCKS into girls for fun. Weird fun. Sinning fun. Lenny says they stick their COCKS into the girl's CUNT (he said it: not me), and if they aren't careful they make a baby together. Jesus Christ must have a COCK and he must have stuck it—
   Our father, who art in heaven, hallowed be thy name . . .
3. When kids torture Nellie Parker, I don't stop them. I never join in or laugh or even smile at what they say about her and what they do to her, but I also don't shout, Hey, quit it! I don't shout, She's never done anything to you, has she? So what if she is sick a lot and is fat and ugly and maybe she should wash her hair and

buy nicer clothes. You're still being mean and nasty, and Missus Grundel and Father Ferguson and the Pope and probably even the Queen all think it's wrong to treat a kid that way.

What are you saying? asks Mom in the car. Nothing, I answer, my cheeks warm. How was school today? she says. Fine, I reply.

Stuff That Mom Says Is Bad But Really Isn't

1. Shooting an arrow into the Smiths' pool. Dad buys me a bow and arrow and a target, called a bull's-eye. Mom says it isn't safe to shoot in our backyard. Dad says the target is huge: I can't possibly miss. The arrow goes partway into the deck, not the pool, so it isn't a serious mistake. I could sneak over and pull it out, but Mom makes me knock on their door. Missus Smith says I could have killed someone. She says I'm not Davy Crockett anymore.

2. Talking George into breaking Floyd-the-garbageman's window. We're playing Dare You. Dare you to pee in your mom's flower bed, says George. Easy, I answer, unzipping my pants. Dare you to throw a rock at Floyd's window, I say to him. That's not fair, he replies. It might break. My mom's flowers might die, I say back. George picks up a rock. His first two throws aren't hard and, besides, they hit brick. His third throw bounces off the glass. Did it, he says. Toad could throw harder than that,

I answer. And he's barely four.

The smash is scary—*crash!* goes the window—but also great. Mom comes out. Look what George did, I tell her. I didn't do a thing.

3. Killing insects on the driveway with a basketball. We play to ten. George, who can't bounce the ball, rolls it at the bugs and mostly misses. Jimmy can kill five ants in a row before the ball bounces away. I'm not as good, so I drop the ball, kill and catch, drop the ball, kill and catch. Ant jam covers my fingers. Beetle smear bloodies the ball. Toad likes to play, even though Mom asks him not to kill. He wipes out anthills with his feet.

More Weird Stuff at School

1. Jimmy runs over to me at recess and says that Jerry Ekhorn took a dare from a Grade Five boy and peed into an open manhole on Bayview Avenue. Kids say that as soon as Jerry zipped his fly and bolted, a man wearing a construction helmet climbed out of the hole. Now the man is in the yard, looking for the boy who did it.

Back in the classroom, Sister Mary Wyatt's voice comes on the loudspeaker. She asks for the boy or boys who committed the unspeakable act during recess to get up from their desks this instant. Do that, says the principal, and your punishment will be adjusted accordingly. As soon as she is finished, kids start to whisper and stare at Lenny. I didn't do anything! says Lenny, looking disappointed.

(Jerry is in the other class.) Missus Grundel says, Shhh, children, and reads us a book, but she keeps glancing over at the speaker, as if Sister Mary is suddenly going to appear in it and say: Hello, my pretty. Sure enough, a minute later the principal is back on. Would all male students from Grade Three up to Grade Six report to the gym, she orders. No excuses. No exceptions. I watch Missus Grundel but she only says, Okay, boys, form a line. Hey, asks Billy Neary, how come only us? Do as you're told, answers our teacher. As we march down the hallway, Jimmy makes a joke: If it had been a girl, she'd have fallen in!

A man in an orange outfit stands next to Sister Mary Wyatt. He holds a hard hat. His boots are muddy. The principal watches us as we walk past, sliding the beads of her rosary through her fingers, like she is counting sinful kids. This is Mister Giano, she announces. A child in this gymnasium has just insulted him in the worst possible way. He wants to look each and every one of you in the eye and see if you can still keep lying to him and to me and to God. Grade Threes first, she says. Up against the wall.

I'm third in line and Jimmy is sixth. Jerry Ekhorn is tenth, and he is already close to bawling. Mister Giano steps up to the first kid, John Sealy, and says: You do that to me, son? John shakes his head. No sir, he answers. His voice cracks and older kids laugh. Sister Mary clacks her rosary. Everyone else look straight ahead! she orders. Is all right, Sister, says Mister Giano. No boy going to lie to my face. When he stops at me, a shudder runs through my body. Look into my eyes, son, he says. Mister Giano's eyes are brown with red flecks in the white parts. His brows are dark and nearly meet in the middle. No sir, I answer in a small voice. Honest.

He asks two more boys before he notices Jerry, who is sobbing and sliding down the wall. Mister Giano pulls him back up and says something I can't hear. Jerry nods and answers, Sorry, sorry. Sister Mary Wyatt orders two teachers to bring Jerry Ekhorn down to her office. We all see the snot dribbling from his nose; we all see the stain around his fly. Mister Giano asks the teachers to leave the boy alone. I satisfied, Sister Mary, he says. This child, he already punished. You are a good Christian, Mister Giano, replies the principal. He smiles for the first time. You respect my wish, Sister? he asks. You have my word, she answers, not smiling back.

2. Jerry gets punished anyway. Twice in two weeks, both times with the strap. Before the second strapping, Sister Mary Wyatt enters our class without knocking and asks Missus Grundel if Jerry Ekhorn was involved in the spitball fight in the boys' bathroom. Missus Grundel asks if they can please talk in the corridor. We have no secrets in my school, replies the principal. Answer the question. Our teacher glares at Sister Mary almost the same way she does at misbehaving kids. Yes he did, Sister, she says slowly, but so did several other— Sister Mary crosses the hallway to Missus Gallagher's class. Down to the office, young man, we all hear her say.

3. I keep thinking I should apologize to Missus Grundel for picking my nose. I know it happened ages ago. I know

she's already scolded other kids for doing more yucky stuff—farts and burps, mostly—and made us listen to the nurse talk about personal hygiene. But how she looked at me! How she frowned! *I'm disappointed, Charlie*, said her eyes. *You're not the good boy I thought you were.*

Goofy Stories From Catechism Class

1. Satan used to be an angel in heaven. An important one, with wide wings and keys to all the rooms. He became too greedy, though, so God kicked him out. God wanted to get rid of Satan, but he also needed someone to run hell. Dad says you need good men to look after your branch operations. The farther from head office the plant is, the more competent the manager should be. Satan was nasty and cold-hearted and scared everyone to death: the perfect choice, says Dad. Also, if God hired the devil, he wouldn't have to worry about health benefits. That's an important consideration. For a guy who won't go to church, my father sure knows a lot about religion. Actually, he told Mom he'd go to mass again on the day hell froze over and Lucifer took up hockey. An eternity of hockey? said Mom. Now that *would* be damnation.

   He laughed. She laughed. Weird.

   (I've been watching my parents more. The way they tease each other. The way he kisses her on the forehead when he gets home and sometimes wraps himself around her from behind. The way they dance together in the kitchen if the radio is playing a snappy song, and laugh upstairs late at night, when they think I'm asleep.)

2. People who aren't Catholic, or aren't religions that Father Ferguson calls *almost* Catholic, don't think Jesus was the son of God. They think he was just a man who got hung on a cross. Father Ferguson says we should respect these other religions but also feel sorry for the people who believe them, because they haven't seen the truth and the light and the way of our Lord. They're in trouble, though not like the people in countries where they don't believe in God at all, and instead drop to their knees before statues of fat men in pyjamas, and think that once we die we don't go to heaven or hell. They think we come back to life as monkeys in jungles. Birds in trees. Ants in the sand. They think, says Father during one class, his glasses steamy and his jowls turkey, that God's children, made in his own image, return to this earth as grunting pigs and scaly fish and teeming vermin! Such nonsense. Such ignorance. As if the Lord were so thoughtless. As if he cared so little for his own creations.

3. Jesus had a terrible time at Easter. He had to be kissed by Judas, who was another man. Then he had to carry a cross up a hill so soldiers could nail him to it and put a crown of thorns on his head and stab him in the gut. Then, he had to die. I also have an awful time during the holidays. Mom makes us give something up for Lent. Last year, when I was nuts, I offered to not eat chocolate for forty days and forty nights. I nearly died. I cheated once

or twice. This year I said I'd give up vegetables, heh heh, and then added: Seriously, how about no Bugs Bunny on Saturdays? Seriously, answered Mom, how about no television at all? Come on, Mom, I said, I'm not a priest! Heh heh, she said, running her hand through my brushcut hair. I ended up missing five weekends of cartoons. Lent is bad, but Good Friday is worse. We spend the afternoon at the church listening to the story of the crucifixion. There isn't a special dinner afterwards either or any treats. Finally, though, it's Easter Sunday. Jesus comes back to life and we hunt for eggs—Wait for me! says Toad as we race around the house—and then carry our baskets to the basement, where we eat chocolate bunnies and watch kids' shows until lunch. Mom makes ham and potatoes, and we always talk about Ham-the-turkey. I didn't rush off and puke, says Debbie. I just *said* I did.

Bad Words I've Learned But Wish I Hadn't

1. Cunt
2. Retard
3. Parker the pig, Parker the pig!

How to Stop Bad Words and Ideas From Going Into Your Brain

1. Never play in the schoolyard. Better, don't go to school at all: kids whisper things right in class.

2. Talk only to your mom. If she hears you say a bad word, she grabs a bar of soap. Or talk to a priest. They work for God and will report back—they're not snitching: just doing their jobs—if you swear. For sure, don't talk to your dad, especially if he's in the basement fixing the washing machine. Damn it to hell, he says. Also, Jesus H. Christ! (For a guy who never goes to church, he sure mentions Jesus a lot.) Don't even talk to your big sister or little brother. They both pick up all kinds of bad language, and it isn't always me who teaches Toad, honest. I give you my word.

3. Ask God for help in confession.

Why I Play With Toad in May

1. Jimmy has to stay home and help his mom. I go over to the house once, but Missus Reilly is sleeping and the baby is sleeping and Jimmy can only whisper to me through the screen door.

2. We give my GI Joe, who died in Vietnam, a funeral. First we put him in a coffin—half a milk carton—and march from the back porch out to the yard. Toad wants to hold the flag, which is a pillowcase on a stick, and I say okay, as long as he does the special march—one foot up, one foot down. Mom says there is a funeral song for dead soldiers, but she can't remember the melody. I purt "Ca-na-da" on my fist trumpet and he sings *Ca-na-da / Wee luuv theee* as we cross the yard to the sandbox. I watched a

funeral on TV last night. Soldiers wore black suits and white caps and shot at the clouds with their rifles. An American flag was folded on the coffin; airplanes blasted overhead, leaving smoke tails in the sky. I put GI Joe in the hole and Toad and I pick up our guns. *Pow pow pow* he says. Got one! Not killing shots, I explain. A twenty-one gun salute. But then I look up and see an enemy plane swooping down to drop bombs on a village, bombs that blow up houses and turn trees into matches, all yellow and red and burning; and suddenly I forget about the funeral and dive for cover in the bushes. Run for it! I tell Toad. *Rat-tat-tat-tat!* roars my machine gun.

Good work, Lieutenant, I say, once the battle is over. Thanks, Captain Charlie, he answers. Not captain, I correct him. Colonel Charlie Foran.

We also play spacemen together. Not Dad's dumb stories: real imaginary space adventures. In the winter our ship was a tent in the playroom. We had to pretend the ceiling was a sky of planets and stars. We had to pretend we were miles above the earth. Once, after an Apollo ship was launched on TV, Toad and I made Dad drive to Parkview Park. The spaceship was cold and hard and the wind whipped snow at us. Toad wouldn't even climb the ladder. I wanted to squeeze into the ball at the top—it's shaped like the globe in the classroom—but I kept slipping on the metal. I also banged my chin. Now that it's spring, the ship will be ready and waiting. I can bike to the park by myself. Mom says I'm old enough.

3. If our baseball goes over the fence into the Macgreevys'

yard, he'll get it. We make sure that their dog, Beatrix, isn't around. Then I lift Toad onto the railing and help him down with a push. The back door to their house is behind another fence. The yard has trees, bushes and a shed. If I have to collect the ball I always sneak behind a tree, check for a Macgreevy or Beatrix, then race to a bush. I never run in the open. I never forget the danger. Toad doesn't know any better, though, and he heads straight for the spot. Help me, he says back at the fence. Throw the ball first, I answer. He usually does that—he *is* only four—and then I smile and say, Got you now, Toad.

Mister Macgreevy is an ogre, I tell him. They can smell children from a mile away. Know what happens if he catches you in his yard? What? says my brother, his eyes huge. He'll drop you into a pit so deep you can't see the bottom, even with a flashlight. Mister Macgreevy hides the pit under pretend grass. He'll pull the grass off and— Help! begs Toad. Fee, fi, fo, fum, I say, I smell the poo of a little boy's bum. He's coming, Toad. Hear the porch door opening? Hear his footsteps over the stones? The poor kid is bawling now and rattling the fence. He's also calling for his mom. Shut up, I say, punching the wire. Or else I'll tell on you. I'll tell Mom that—

CHARLIE, she calls from the porch. WHAT ARE YOU DOING TO YOUR LITTLE BROTHER?

(Remember what I said? she asks me, once I've spent another afternoon in my room. He looks up to you. He wants to *be* you. No he doesn't, I correct her. He wants to be an animal doctor.)

Why I Haven't Seen Grandma Lately

1. Mom says we've been busy.
2. Dad says we'll visit her soon.
3. I have seen her, but only when the phone rings at night and I wake up and there she is, floating at the foot of my bed. Grandma Ruthie has wings and a halo. Her hair, more gold than red, is down to her shoulders; her neck and arms are smooth, before she turned wrinkly. She isn't the grandma with the braided hair and butterfly glasses. She's the one in the photo in our living room. That grandma is seated on a couch with a grand-baby in her arms. Next to her is Grandpa. He is wearing a tie and suit with a hankie in his pocket and a cigarette between his fingers; she has on a pretty dress, earrings and a necklace, fancy shoes. He is proud: her cheeks are pink from smiling. He is handsome and she is beautiful and they are Ruthie and Charlie Foran, my grandparents, my father's mom and dad, which means they must also be . . . I mean . . . he must be? . . . mustn't he? . . . That is the grandma at my bed.

   Know who the baby is? Know who is making them so happy?

Our Visit to Grandpa's Farm

1. Are you the boy who keeps using my name? he asks me at the door. He's still the photo in our living room. His

hair is still silver and his moustache is still thin. His clothes still stink of cologne. You look like your mom, he says. My mom is French, I answer for no reason, except that I'm uncomfortable. And your dad is Ottawa Valley Irish, he says. A natural match. Debbie comes over and gives him a kiss. Your sister is a dead ringer for Barb, says Grandpa, touching her hair. Who's Barb? I ask. He smokes his cigarette and drinks from his glass. Smoke shoots from his nostrils. Ice cubes clink. She's my daughter, he finally replies. Your only aunt. Oh yeah, I say. Aunt Barb. That's her, says Grandpa.

Later, we're in the TV room at the side of the house. Mom and Debbie are helping Shirley—Who's she? asked Toad, forcing Mom to say *shhh*—in the kitchen. Dad has taken Mike to the barn. I sit on the stool he uses for his feet. Did you really get your nose blown off during the war? I ask him. The bridge I was *on* got blown up, answers Grandpa. A plank ripped the nose from my face. And you broke your back too? I say, remembering what Dad told me. That was another time, he replies. Blackout on the base. Couldn't see the hand in front of me. My batman cuts the lights on our jeep and proceeds to drive it into the side of a truck. I'm thrown clear. His head is severed from his neck. Guess I got lucky by comparison, eh? he says, laughing his big deep laugh, which I definitely remember from our last visit (also maybe from dreams). The laugh relaxes my shoulders. If your nose was torn off, I say, feeling comfortable enough to look at him, what's that below your eyes? Ah, says Grandpa, pulling me onto his lap. I'm too big to sit there, but I don't mind. Up close, his eyes are watery and his cheeks are lined with blue veins. Hairs grow not only on his head and above his lip but between his eyebrows. Doctors rebuilt it, answers Grandpa, using skin from my backside. My surprise must show. That's right, Charlie Foran, he says. Your grandfather has an ass for a nose! His laugh is a roar now and he winds up coughing into a hankie. The handkerchief is also the one in the photograph, neatly folded, letters stitched in black (CJF, I think, though the lines are swirly).

Want to touch it? he asks.

His nose is soft and wobbly and the holes are tiny, nearly shut. No cartilage up there, he explains. Sock me one and I'll hardly feel it. Were you a GI Joe in the war? I ask. No GI Joes in the Canadian army, he replies. Only first-rate soldiers. Finest combat troops in the world. Okay, I say, suddenly nervous again. Your dad's old man was an acting general at the end of the war, he adds, looking past me to the window. Retired a full colonel. Colonel Charlie Foran, he says. That's me. That's you too.

Can I, one more time? I ask him. You bet, he answers. I'm pinching Grandpa's nose and laughing so hard I'm almost falling off his lap when Dad enters the room with Toad. Look at this boy, says Grandpa. A real nose licker. Would have made a great officer, eh?

Dad smiles.

2. His pool is still empty from the winter. I ask if I can climb down the ladder. Why? says Mom. I just want to,

I reply. Do you remember playing in that empty pool in California on the day President Kennedy died? she asks. Of course I don't, Mom, I answer. I was only three. She tells me to be careful. I drop onto the floor. *Aaaah*, I say, and *Heeey!* I draw circles in the muck with my boots and watch birds shoot past. The sky looks different from below: taller and more blue, each cloud its own shape. If they were stars, I think to myself, they'd probably have names. Every cloud is different and so is every snowflake and every person, every kid. Since I can't see much from the bottom and hear only the wind, the farm soon disappears. Bye, Mom and Dad and Debbie and Toad. Bye, Grandpa and Shirley. Maybe I do start to remember the pool in California. Maybe I do start to remember nearly drowning in Ottawa.

Someone calls to me and I jump. A man stands at the rim. I shield my eyes. Look, Dad, I call back. I'm the first boy to reach the centre of the earth! When he doesn't speak, I pretend to swim, moving my arms and taking deep breaths and then—who knows why?—I shout, Help, help, I'm drowning! Again, the person doesn't answer. Dad? I ask, my stomach tightening. Is that—? It's Charlie, Charlie, he replies. Don't you know who I am?

3. At lunch Toad asks Shirley a dumb question. Are you my grandma? he says. Shirley grins and answers in her gravel voice: If you want me to be, Mike. Debbie, who wears a dress and has a bow in her hair, bangs her fork on her plate. She's *not* our grandmother, she says. She's just some lady. Now, kids, says Grandpa, wiping his

mouth with a napkin. I think I'm more than just some lady to you children, replies Shirley, lighting a cigarette. (The match goes out twice.) But what does it matter? Shirley, says Mom. You know they don't— Debbie runs crying from the room. Toad says, Humph, and folds his arms. How's your steak, Charlie? asks Grandpa. Delicious, I answer.

In the car Dad puffs his pipe and listens to the radio. Debbie asks him to quiz her on the provinces and states but he says, Not today, kids. I ask him to sing "King of the Road" or "Hey Good Lookin." Mom answers, It's been a long day for everyone. Then she asks Debbie if she'd like to have a sleepover with Grandma Ruthie next weekend. Sure! says my sister. Mom looks at me, worried that I'm upset, but I smile. Can you buy me some cloth handkerchiefs? I ask her. The kind you wash and fold and sew your initials on. What's wrong with Kleenex? she says. Not dapper enough, I reply. Excuse me? says Mom. I repeat the word. Hear that, Dave? she says. Charlie thinks Kleenex aren't dapper enough!

What's that? asks Dad.

Weird Things at School (Last Ones)

1. Jimmy and I are laughing about something—okay, Mister Woo's funny English: You boys eat lot of choco-late, get big fat big, okay?—when Missus Grundel, who has already sent Billy into the hallway and has told us,

Don't push your luck, children, walks down to our desks and says, That's it. Jimmy stands up—this isn't his first time—but I don't move. Couldn't I just sit on my hands for a few minutes? I ask my teacher. Are you deciding my punishments for me now, child? she answers, not really angry. Leave the door open behind you.

Billy Neary isn't in the hallway. Without using words, I ask Jimmy where Billy has gone. He shrugs. Just then the intercom beeps. Billy Neary is in the principal's office, Missus Grundel, says the secretary. Sister Mary Wyatt is having a word with him. Thanks, Missus Stevenson, answers our teacher. She pokes her head into the corridor. Behave and I'll let you back in soon, she tells us.

Sister Mary Wyatt's office is down the hall. Hard to believe I once thought she was a cute penguin. She isn't cute: she's cruel and loves to see kids in pain. Except for the gentle way she treats Nellie Parker and her smart rule about British Bulldog (a boy nearly ripped my arm off last week), she's the worst principal in Willowdale, maybe in all Canada. Even the way she punishes children who've been sent into the hallway isn't fair. Everyone knows she hates climbing the stairs. Everyone knows kids in the classrooms on the second floor don't get caught as often.

I press my shoulders to the wall. Jimmy, though, acts crazy. Not only does he march back and forth across the floor, he also flutters his fingers through the air. What are you doing? I whisper to him. He keeps moving his fingers, as if he's— Don't you remember? he asks.

Missus Grundel clears her throat.

Jimmy stands next to me, his smile wide. He keeps on fluttering. He keeps on playing Miss Malone's piano.

2. Our teacher begins class on the first day in June with an announcement. Nellie Parker won't be returning to school until September, says Missus Grundel, staring out the window. She starts her next sentence twice. Even though Nellie left early last Friday because of the things a child wrote on her desk, she says, it doesn't mean she is quitting. You haven't defeated her. You haven't chased her away. Missus Grundel turns to us. Nellie is genuinely sick, she adds in a softer voice. If only you children understood. If only you understood what you are capable of doing . . .

Darn, says Lenny in the yard. No more Nellie cooties.

3. We play British Bulldog at lunch. I'm one of two kids still free. These days, the last one uncaptured gets piled on, even though he's supposed to be the winner. Boys form a line across the field. Jay Kerry, who'd be in Grade Six if he hadn't flunked last year, shouts, One, two, three—go! and then adds: You're both dead! What happens next is so weird I almost trip over my own feet. As I zig-zag up the field, dodging some kids while pushing others away with my arms, I suddenly start to think about Nellie Parker. About last Friday, when students surrounded her in the yard and sang the Parker-the-pig rhyme. About watching her read the words someone scrawled on top of her desk with a red pencil. About Missus Grundel

helping her stand up—Get up, child, she said softly—and wrapping her arm around Nellie's shoulders. About Nellie's face as she walked up the— *Wham*, I get hit. Slowed down. *Wham*, one Grade Four grabs my shirt and another sticks out his leg. My chin slams into the ground. My left arm is pinned. First, a boy jumps on my back. Then they all pile on. Get off me, I hear myself shouting, though no one hears. I'm not Nellie Parker!

Why There's No Way I Saw Allan Yesterday

1. No curtains on his house. No car in his driveway. A FOR SALE sign still on the lawn.
2. Mom thinks his mother moved Allan back to Sudbury or North Bay. What about the dad? I ask. There is no father, she answers. He went away when Allan was very young. (Did I know this?) You mean he died? I say. No, she replies, looking straight into my eyes. He left his wife and son. Left to go to work, you mean? I ask, though that doesn't sound right. Mom shakes her head. Grown-ups don't always stay together, she says. Even when there are children involved.

   I also ask Graham Nester about Allan. He rubs his chin. For a second I decide that Graham looks a little like my grandpa. (He definitely looks like Mr. Magoo.) Then he opens his mouth. *Och*, he says. *Not ull bairns share equal in Gud's bounty.* Okay, I answer, scratching Robbie between the ears.

3. A family with two girls live in the Nicolson house now. The Bumpity is a paved street. The field is the Willowtree Estates. All of which means it's impossible for a tall boy in torn jeans and a T-shirt to walk over one afternoon while I'm playing ball hockey by myself—*Roar!* shouts the crowd after each amazing goal—and say, How are you doing? Fine, I answer. Think Pete wants to come out and play? the tall boy asks, pointing to the house. I knock my stick against the curb. You still . . . , I begin. I mean, you still bite your nails? He shows me his hands. Sometimes I also pick at the skin around the nails until it bleeds, he says. My mom says it's because I'm anxious. What does anxious mean? I ask. He shrugs. I'm not really from here, you know, adds the boy. We're from a small town up north. It's a way different place, eh?

Before I know what to answer—for some reason, I think of my cousin Luc—he's walking away. Pete Nicolson's mom and dad moved him off the street more than a year ago, I manage to say. And you left too!

Sorry about your dad, I add in my head.

Things That Happen in June

1. Another king dies in America. Mom is quiet all day. Something terrible has happened again, kids, she says. When Dad gets home from work, they hug at the stove. Remember the last time? asks Mom. Remember watching the television in California? Sure I do, answers Dad. That

poor family must be cursed. I have a question about the poor family. Does being a king who is now dead mean going away from your family? Going away, despite the children? I also have a question about California. In our photo box is a picture of me and Debbie standing with Mickey Mouse. We're members of the Mickey Mouse Club. We're in Disneyland. I sort of remember Disneyland and I sort of remember shaking hands with Mickey. Also, now that Mom has told me, I for sure remember playing in an empty pool and seeing my Grandpa smile down at me from the top. But living in California, where Dad says it's always warm and you can pick oranges off trees? Where Toad was almost born and another American king was killed? I don't remember that place at all.

2. Trudeaumania wins. Buttons come off jackets and signs off lawns. Pierre Elliott, as Mom calls him, becomes our president. Prime minister, corrects Dad. We don't have presidents. Not even killed ones? I ask. Especially not killed ones, he answers. Do we have a pope? Of course, says Mom. He's above the clock in Missus Grundel's room. Is he the pope of all Canada? He's the pope of all Catholics, she replies. In Canada and around the world. Is the Queen the queen of all Catholics as well? She's the Englishman's queen, says Dad. But also ours? He frowns. Not mine, he finally answers. Maybe Pierre Elliott should be our pope and queen and president *and* prime minister, I say. That'd be simpler.

Smart kid, says Dad, ruffling my hair.

3. I apologize to Missus Grundel for picking my nose in class. Yes, Charlie? she says when I stop at her desk, hiding my shaking hands behind my back. It won't happen again, I blurt. And you know why? Slow down, says my teacher. What won't happen again? Because my mom is buying me cloth hankies that I can keep in my pockets, I continue. That way, I can pull them out any time and . . . you know . . . Ah, says Missus Grundel. I see what you're saying. My grandpa uses cloth handkerchiefs, I explain. He folds them into his pants or his suit pocket. I'm going to do the same, as soon as Mom buys me some.

Good boy, says my teacher.

1969

Next morning I bomb over to Parkview Park. Mom asks me to eat some breakfast, but I can't wait. Toad, now called Mike, begs to come, but I say, Forget it. I want to be the first and I want to do it on my own. My legs are wobbly from staying up so late—midnight, because history was being made—and I forget to brush my teeth. As soon as I turn the corner I know I'm in luck: the park is empty. I ride up on the grass and ditch my bike. Jimmy and I have already done the launch twice, and Toad—Mike, I mean—went on some spacewalks with me yesterday, while we waited for the lunar module to land. What's left is the incredible part. The part that changed the world. The part that points to a bright future. I climb the ladder and crouch inside the hull. On the ground below are two beer bottles. Up in the globe is a gym sock. The sky is bright. The sun burns. Already I can feel my hair gluing to my forehead and my toes squishing inside my shoes. Already I'm sweaty and smelly and my breath probably stinks. My heart jumps. My palms stick. Finally, I turn around and begin. In my mind is the picture on TV. The astronauts wore heavy suits and backpacks *but, being in space, they still bounced. Though I'm in shorts and a T-shirt, I also weigh ninety pounds. First rung, I feel the pull. Second rung on the ladder, my shoe slips off the metal and I nearly fall. THAT'S ONE SMALL STEP FOR MAN, said Neil Armstrong last night, ONE GIANT LEAP FOR MANKIND. I say it too, hesitating as I touch the surface.*

What happened at school was this. In class one day Brenda Deane passed a note to Joanne Kuri that Missus Delmer almost saw. Joanne then slipped a note to Jimmy, which I'm positive our teacher did see, though she didn't say anything. Jimmy, who isn't allowed to sit next to me, raised his hand to sharpen his pencil. Walking past my desk, he whispered that we were to meet at the back corner of the yard at noon. Some kids must have heard him, since by the time he and I started across to the baseball diamond we were being trailed by half the class, including sucks like Joey Rossi and snitches like Suzy Garner. Brenda and Joanne were waiting. Joanne said, Run for it, and the four of us bolted. Brenda took the lead. She dipsy-doodled like a British Bulldog champion and we wound up alone in the corner above Bayview Avenue. Brenda smiled at me and Joanne smiled at Jimmy, and we were all smiles and giggles and pink cheeks. Then Joanne kissed Jimmy on the lips. Smack, without warning. He grinned and closed his eyes. I was watching this, feeling kind of fluttery, when Brenda moved in. I turned to be ready for her, but I also did the same as Jimmy. She must have closed her eyes as well, because we missed. I kissed her nose. She kissed my chin. Brenda's nose was amazing. She's got orange hair and freckles and eyes as big as Wagonwheels. Everyone says she's pretty. Everyone says she runs faster than any boy.

Chase you, she said. Jimmy was already flying and Joanne was already after him. I waited for a second—this was the start of something, I knew—then took off. Checking over my shoulder, I saw Brenda right behind me, her curls bouncing.

Watch, Toad, I say, holding up his bear, which he never plays with anymore. Bear can't stand it when this happens. I smash the animal against the wall. Ouch, ouch—he just *hates* that.

Stop, says Mike, grabbing at it.

And Bear really gets annoyed when this happens, I continue. I open the closet door and stick its head in. Geewhillikers, I say, whacking the door against Bear. Does that sting!

I'm going to tell Mom.

Suck.

Give me Bear.

Come and get him, I answer, crossing to the hallway. (He and I have moved into Deb's old bedroom upstairs.) Mike follows me out. As soon as he's near, I drop the animal down the stairs. Bear bounces on most steps and crashes into the front door at the bottom.

I'm five now, says my brother. My name is Mike.

Okay.

Want to slide down on our bums?

That's for kids.

He's already on the top step. To get ahead, I shove him and shoot down on my rear. Incredible how fast I move. Incredible how hard I land. My head jerks back. My mouth stings.

You okay? asks Mike.

Of course I am, TOAD.

In the bathroom I spit blood mixed with phlegm. It dribbles like candlewax down the inside of the sink. At the hole, the ooze stops. I touch it, make it jiggle. The gunk sits there until I turn on the tap.

Are you limping, Charlie? asks Mom.

My leg, I answer, rubbing my thigh. I hurt it playing hockey.

When?

A while ago. It acts up now and then.

She looks at me. Weren't you just watching TV with your father? she says.

A movie about the war Grandpa fought in.

Anyone get shot in it?

It was a war, Mom, I say. Of course they did.

Anyone shot in the leg?

Happens all the time, I explain.

Have you ever really looked at your dad? I haven't, until now. He's who you'll look like once you grow up. He's you, basically, only maybe less so if he has a bristly chin and tons of freckles and a gut so huge you can sit on it, like a camel's hump, though if you do that after Christmas dinner, when he and Jack Pierce are lying on the living room floor, eyes shut and hands across chests, snores snapping the air; if you choose that moment to jump on your dad's stomach, he may say *ooooh!* and rush to the bathroom. He's also *his* dad, of course, though to be honest I don't see it. Some fathers on our street walk to work or ride the bus. Jimmy's dad actually drives a bus, as his job. My dad puts on a suit and tie and climbs into our Mercury. Bobby Avery says a Mercury is a big shot's car. Bobby also says having an office with a secretary and a couch means you're a boss. I ask Dad if he has these things. He says he does, except for the couch. Two out of three is still pretty good, I figure. My dad, the big shot. I'm darn proud of him.

Girls are totally gross, said George on the way home from school. They pee through holes in their behinds and have a slit instead of a penis and when they grow up their breasts get huge and full of milk.

Yuck, I agreed.

Could you imagine having such a disgusting body?

Not a chance.

I'd never kiss a girl, he said. Would you?

Don't think so, I answered slowly.

Joey Rossi said he saw Jimmy Reilly kiss Joanne Kuri behind the baseball diamond.

Jimmy hates girls.

Suzy Garner saw it too.

She's a—

We stopped talking as we passed Finch Avenue Public. Kids were racing out the gate onto Estelle. We knew a few of the Grade Fours, including Keith Healy's friends over on Dunforest and boys from the Willowtree Estates, but we never said much more than hi to them.

You ever get a boner? asked George.

Not really.

Lenny says he gets one every day. He says he'll show it to us.

When?

Tomorrow. At lunch.

Both of us dropped our hands to our zippers.

Lenny will do anything, I said.

Jimmy Reilly kissed Joanne Kuri.

Not a chance.

Girls *are* yucky, I'm still sure. Except for Brenda Deane. She has Wagonwheel (or Joe Louis) eyes. Her hair is as orange as, well, a real orange; her freckles are like splotches of paint on paper. Her teeth are whiter than . . . as white as . . . they're really white. She runs faster than any boy.

God is stupid, I say in the bathtub. To make certain no one hears me, I sink under the water. All I do then is whisper the words and they sound as if I am God's voice on television. GOD IS STUPID, the voice booms. HE'S A DORK.

Blasphemy means thinking or saying sinful things about the Lord. At school blasphemy would get me strapped. In my own bathroom it should make God want to show me who's boss. Piranhas from the drain. Lightning out the shower nozzle. While I wait to see what will happen, I watch the tip of my penis bob in the water. It's soft and pink and I like to touch it. If I pull the skin back, a shiver starts near my belly button and spreads. If I keep pulling, I have to close my eyes to stop the dizziness. Ten minutes go by. I push and pull. I squeeze. Finally, I admit that my sister is right. God isn't paying attention to what we do. He's way up on top of the universe, or maybe even farther out—at school, we learned that there are loads of universes with loads of suns and moons—and probably has no idea that I'm blasphemizing his name. Debbie said God is a lifeguard in charge of a beach. We're grains of sand along the shore. One grain equals a boy or girl. One grain! No wonder he couldn't care less.

Standing in a corner of the dining room as punishment— Lucky your father isn't here, says Mom—for using the word *shit* to describe the taste of fried liver, I slip into the closet and close the door. Amazing how dark it gets. Amazing how cramped. Last summer I slept in my *tante* Cecile's house for a week. The bedroom had a slanted ceiling and bunkbeds built into the walls. I had the top bunk and, if I stretched, I could touch the ceiling or hold my hand in the light that painted a stripe on the floor. Trains went past all night. Stuff didn't rattle—the tracks were blocks away—but the *chunk-chunk chunk-chunk* woke me up, along with the *whoo-whoo* of the whistle. Dad said the conductor had to sound the whistle in populated areas. Freight trains, he explained, on their way up to Port Arthur or down to Sudbury. I felt tiny every time one rattled on the tracks. I felt lonely with each whistle. The train had come from one place and was going to another. I watched light flicker against the wall. The train moved through the dark. I could hear it moving inside my head.

Mom and I spend fifty-two minutes searching the garden for Timothy-the-turtle. It's only November, but she isn't taking chances. Timothy is American—Mom and Dad found him trying to cross a highway on a trip last fall— and isn't used to Canadian weather. Home for half the year is a shoe closet. Home for the other half is somewhere in the rockery. His shell is grey-green, like rocks. He almost never moves or pokes his head out. He definitely doesn't whistle.

We won't find him, I say.

Is a turtle's shell his body? He lives in it the way we live in our houses. I know you can't suck Timothy out of his shell; I know he's attached. Still, either it is his home and he ought to be able to leave it when he wants, or else his head and neck and his four legs are actually his brain, his imagination—the stuff inside that you can't see, but is important.

Found him! says Mom. She lifts up a small rock. I knock on the shell.

Anybody home? I call.

What happened in the yard one incredible day was this. Guys were heading over to the baseball diamond to see Lenny's boner. I wasn't interested, and Matt Kelly told me afterwards that Lenny chickened out when the on-duty teacher, Mister Harkness, started across the field. Jimmy and I were behind the gym, waiting for Jill Taggert to report. She'd taken a message to Joanne and Brenda, saying that I liked Brenda but I didn't love her, and that Jimmy *almost* loved Joanne. Jill was returning from the kissing corner, where the other girls stood, to tell us that Joanne almost loved Jimmy back but that Brenda for sure *did* love me, and if I didn't say I loved her she was going to chase me all over the yard. I was thinking of an answer when some Grade Seven kids hung a Grade Five boy on the volleyball pole using his underpants. The boy started to kick and cry. By the time Mister Harkness jogged over to the court, a different group had tied the prettiest girl in Grade Six, Mary Ellen Kearney, to another pole using a jump rope. They were dancing Indian around her, slapping their fingers over their mouths to make the *wo-ah wo-ah* and shouting that she was a witch burning at the stake, when Sister Mary Wyatt came rocketing out of the middle doors without a coat on. I'd never seen her run before. Her cheeks puffed with air. She took short shuffle steps. Still, the principal moved so fast that the boys didn't notice her. She grabbed one of the Macmillans by the ear and said, Stop! Then she called to Mister Harkness. He gave up trying to free the underwear boy and rushed over, change rattling in his pocket. Mister Harkness promised Sister Mary he'd bring the culprits down to the office. Go on in, Sister, he added. It's freezing out here.

That afternoon the corridors were as quiet as the church on Good Friday. Everyone listened for the whacks of the strap and the cries of the boys and maybe a shout of No more! or I'm sorry! Everyone wondered who was giving the punishment and how many hits Sister Mary had ordered. Everyone, I bet, felt their own palms sting and their own face burn.

Sister Mary Wyatt spoke on the intercom. The grounds of this school will not be allowed to degenerate into a Lord of the Flies, she said. Not while I am still principal. Not while I—and my staff—can exercise our rightful authority.

Yes, Charlie? said Missus Delmer.

What is a Lord of the Flies?

It's a book.

Oh.

About children who treat each other in a terrible manner, she added with a frown.

Can I borrow it from the library?

Wait until you're older.

But—

Let's do some reading ourselves, shall we? said our teacher, the nicest in the school. She opened *Charlotte's Web* and read to us about a talking pig and a spelling spider. I listened and doodled in my exercise book. I could do that now: draw faces and animals or even just swirling, spinning shapes, and still hear what was being said. Doodling used up only half my attention. It was harder than copying out words but easier than thinking them up and arranging them. I filled in most margins. I also doodled on the backs of spelling quizzes and multiplication tests. Missus Delmer said she liked my doodlings. But she also had no choice except to mark me down for sloppiness. I told her I understood. I'm a southpaw, I explained. My dad says it's a miracle I can write and chew gum at the same time.

Dad took me for a drive last summer to see where the Indians lived outside Blind River. Their town was a road in the woods. The houses were small and had no garages or yards. A lot of them used plastic for windows. A few were missing front doors. People sat on porches watching us. Kids playing in the street stared; dogs chased the car. I looked at the grown-up Indians and the kid Indians and I looked at their houses and suddenly I wanted to stay inside our Mercury. If I'd seen any teepees, it might have been different. If I'd seen anyone wearing moccasins or feathers, dancing and singing *wo-ah wo-ah:* if I'd seen anybody having fun in their Indian clothes and Indian houses I might have asked Dad to stop.

I ate dinner at Jimmy's house the other night. His sister and two brothers are great and his mom is my favourite mother in the world, except for my own. His dad talks like Graham Nester without the *ochs*. Mister Reilly's accent is singsongy and quick and he doesn't move his lips when he speaks. I could listen to him for hours. Missus Reilly also has a neat accent, even though she's Canadian. She always calls me Charles and adds the word *dear*. Come in, Charles dear, says Jimmy's mom. Also: Tell me, dear, how are all your family?

We played Taking Shots in his yard. The net had holes, so we stood it against the back of the house. Our sticks tore up the grass, but Jimmy said it was okay. Mister Reilly came out. Time for me to be heading off, he said. It's eleven minutes and thirty-five seconds after seven, Mister Reilly, I answered. He smiled. And is the watch by any chance new? he asked. Birthday present, I replied. I asked for it. There's a good lad, he said without any lip movement.

Is your dad rich? asked Jimmy once he left.

I don't think so.

I think he is.

Not like Coach Byrne. And Dennis Turner's dad is a doctor. And John Sealy's owns a—

I know, he interrupted, in a way that showed he was angry. But he's still richer than . . . I mean, he's still . . . How come he never goes to church?

Hell hasn't frozen over, I guess.

My dad takes us to St. Pascal's, said Jimmy, not listening to my answer. I'd rather go to Blessed Trinity with other kids from the school.

Is St. Pascal's closer?

It's for pizans and micks, he replied with a shrug.

What's a pizan?

He slapped the ball hard. It hit the dining room window. The window didn't break, but the ball left a smear.

Margaret Mahoney and me want to get married, said Jimmy. Her father owns a shoe company.

What about Joanne Kuri?

We broke up. Two days ago, in the ravine. Her dad fixes toilets as his job.

Were you and her kissing down there?

Of course. So, will you?

His words made me quiet. How come he didn't tell me about the ravine? I might have gone with them. Your uncle is a priest, I said. He can do the marriage.

My uncle lives in Ireland.

I pretended to think. I can't be the priest, I finally said. God is angry with me for calling him stupid.

Why did you—?

It was a test. To see if he was listening.

Has anything bad happened since?

No.

There you go then, said Jimmy, sounding exactly like Mister Reilly. He didn't hear you.

Or he isn't up there.

Sure he is, he said, scoring a goal. We're Catholics. He has to be.

Is Margaret in love with you? I asked.

Jill said she is.

And you said—?

I said I probably was. Jill told Margaret, and she said that probably was good enough.

I missed and hit the back door.

So, will you? he asked again.

In the ravine?

No, stupid—the church.

C'est triste, says Mom on the phone. *Bien, bien triste, Marie. Donne-lui toutes nos pensées.* Noticing me, she switches to English: Yes, the kids are all fine. Charlie's right here, and I know he sends his love to you and Rény. Mom hasn't figured it out yet, but she can't use French to hide her conversations anymore. Twice a week Madame Houde teaches our class about Monsieur et Madame Leduc, their children Henri and Marie-Claire, plus *le chien* Pitou. *Madame Leduc est dans la cuisine*, we repeat together. *Monsieur Leduc est dans le sous-sol.* Twice a week I speak and hear the French language. Some of the words Mom uses we've already learned. *Triste* means sad and *amour* is love. If I wanted to, I could attach those words to what I heard them talking about last night—The mill is closing down, eh? said Dad at the kitchen table: Rény thinks for good this time, she answered, and they're sick with worry—and come up with the story. The connection.

I made a connection last summer. We were in *tante* Marie's kitchen. On the table were salt and pepper shakers, a sugar bowl, plus an apple pie with one slice cut. She and mom were drinking coffee. Have you ever really looked at your mom? I hadn't, until then. Though she looks a lot like her other sisters, I noticed that she and Marie had different faces. When I asked about this, they were amazed. That's a very adult thing to notice, said Mom. (I'm proud of you too, Mom, I almost answered.) She explained that Marie and two other siblings had had a different father. When that man died, my grandmother married again. The second husband was my mom's dad and Marie's step-dad. I finally remembered to ask his name. Robert Fallu, answered Mom. Their mother's name was Hélène Fallu, née Berthelot. Nay? I said. Born, replied Mom. Her maiden name. Were you *née* something else too? I asked. I was Muriel Fallu until I married your father, she said. But Grandma Ruthie is still Ruthie Foran, isn't she? Yes she is, answered Mom quietly. Names can get complicated sometimes. They sure can, I said, leaving it at that. But here is what I was thinking: I'm definitely Charlie Foran, like my grandfather, but until I asked I'd never even heard the name Robert Fallu. Still, wasn't he as much my grandfather as Grandpa is? Shouldn't I look as much like him as my other grandparents? Also, shouldn't I be part Foran, part Fallu: part sad and part *triste*?

Grandma Ruthie is babysitting us tonight. I hug her when she comes in. Her body is all bones: in her shoulders and back, her neck and face. When I kiss her cheek, I kiss a hard bone; when I squeeze her hand, I squeeze thin ones. Once, I picked up a bird that had flown into our front window.

Not thinking, I pressed my finger into its wings, to feel the soft. I heard a tiny crack and the bird died. Every time I hug Grandma, I feel the soft. Every time I smell her perfume, so strong it's a cloud around her, I think of crackings.

You're so grown up now, she says to me at dinner. I hardly recognized you. Mike and I are eating the food Mom left on the stove. (Debbie went out with them. She wore a new dress.) Grandma is smoking a cigarette and drinking orange juice. Can I have some juice? asks Mike, reaching for her glass. You don't want any of this juice, kiddo, she answers, her laugh turning into a cough. After we finish, she gives us each a chocolate bar from her purse. Don't tell your folks, she whispers. She doesn't eat anything herself— she's still sick—but she drinks more juice. At bedtime she says, It sure is a long way up to your new room. Grandma sits on my bed with her eyes closed. Then she asks Mike to come over. I love you kids, she says, trying a double hug. We love you too, Grandma, we answer. No, I *really* love you, she says, kissing me on the cheek. Her eyes are huge and wet and I want to look into them. But she keeps turning away, or else gives us more kisses. Stop squirming, I almost tell her. Instead, Mike says: Don't cry, Grammy. It's because I love you both, she answers.

Am I like my dad when he was nine? I ask her. Exactly like him, she replies. Then you should be able to recognize me easily, I say. Grandma stands up. I hope I get back down those stairs alive, she tells us.

I hold my watch to the window every few minutes. At twelve sixteen, they still aren't home. I hear the *hmmm* of the highway and listen for a train whistle. (George swears that trains pass through Willowdale at night.) I also listen for sounds downstairs, hoping it will be Mom, Dad and Debbie coming in. Something won't let me sleep. Something keeps me alert. At twelve fifty-two the door finally opens and I get up. Mom is on the landing. What are you doing awake? she whispers. When I start down the stairs she glances into the living room, which I can't see, and says, Dave, it's Charlie. Let me help you up, I hear Dad say to someone. Mom climbs a step and steers me into the dining room. Then she gives me a kiss, her eyebrows curving in shock. Into the washroom, she orders. As I turn the corner I notice Dad closing the door to Debbie's room, where Grandma is staying. In the bathroom I stare at my face. Incredible how much lipstick is still on my cheek. Amazing how much it looks like blood. Your pillow must be a mess, says Mom, wiping me with a cloth.

The third time Missus Delmer had to stop reading *Charlotte's Web* to ask Jimmy and Joanne Kuri to quit giggling, she walked down the aisle and said, I'd like you to wait in the hallway, Jimmy Reilly. Jimmy blushed pink, then red, then the grape colour that Lenny Grusa sometimes turns. When he shook his head our teacher said: Excuse me? When he shook it again, even I started to feel embarrassed. You won't stand up? she said. In a minute, he answered in a little kid's voice. Missus Delmer seemed about to lose her temper. If you don't rise this instant, she said, I'll have no choice but to—

Jimmy stood. Strange, he kept his hands pressed against his pants. He also begged our teacher with his eyes. More strange, Missus Delmer ordered him to sit back down again. See me at recess, she added.

He told me the unbelievable story after school. Even though he'd broken up with her, Joanne Kuri had said Jimmy could touch her vagina if she could feel his penis. Right in the classroom! Right during Charlotte and Wilbur! He went first. First he touched her skin and the elastic on her panties. To go farther in, he'd need to pretend that he'd dropped his pencil. And suppose his fingers got stuck down there? Then came Joanne's turn. They both kept their eyes straight ahead as she slid her hand across the seat to his zipper. But instead of just touching, she squeezed. Jimmy thought it was going to hurt. It didn't. She squeezed a second time. Suddenly Joanne yanked her hand back and made a funny sound—half surprise, half fear. Jimmy knew something was wrong. He looked down. At his zipper. At the thing.

A boner, he told me.

Your penis got hard?

You bet.

But there's no bone in it, I said. It's just flappy skin and a squishy sack.

There's a bone, answered Jimmy. Believe me.

Bones are in arms and shoulders and on cheeks, I said. You feel them when you hug someone or share a bed. There's no bone down there.

He shrugged.

You can't marry Margaret now, I said.

Sure I can, he replied. Unless you act like a suck and break your promise.

Touching a girl's vagina is gross, I said.

Jimmy, who shrugs a lot, shrugged again.

The children's librarian calls our house one day to say I've borrowed most of their books. She thinks I'm ready for an adult library card. Mom drives me over that afternoon and a woman who keeps her glasses on a leash around her neck, like Grandma, types my name and address onto a card. Welcome to the adult section, Charlie, she says. You'll never run out of books here. I ask her if I can choose anything. Pretty much, she answers. Can I read *The Lord of All Flies?* I say. The librarian wrinkles her nose. Wait a while for that one, okay? she replies.

In the parking lot I ask Mom if she really is Broadbeam Muriel and if Dad actually is Potbelly Dave. That was just for the party, she says with a laugh. Mom and Dad had a party last Saturday night. I helped pass the invitations out: *The Forans invite all lumberjacks to a . . .* Only people dressed as lumberjacks—striped shirts with suspenders, tuques and rubber boots—could come. Mom made up name tags; Dad invented games. One-handed cigarette rolling was dumb, though the next afternoon, when I told Dad that I was kept awake until two o'clock by laughter (Jack Pierce, mostly), he blamed it. Logrolling was more fun. Dad put two logs on the playroom floor and laid another one across. Lumberjacks had to balance on the rolling pole. I tried it before the party and slipped every time. I wanted to try again on Sunday, but by then the top pole was broken and the floor was covered in paper plates, beer bottles, ashtrays and pieces of paper with the words to lumberjack songs on them. Do all grown-ups act that silly? I ask Mom in the car. Or is it just the crazy Forans and their friends?

She is about to answer when the car screeches to a halt. I fly forward into the windshield. My head bonks glass and I hear a crack. When I sit back, all I can see is snowy fuzz. Mom says something. Ouch, I reply, feeling my forehead. She talks again. Are you okay? she asks, her voice sounding like mission control calling Houston. Okay, I finally answer. The snow melts. The fuzz clears.

The window, Mom, I say. Look!

The windshield has shattered into a thousand Grade Four doodles. Amazing how clear the lines are. Incredible how interesting the shapes. I see a spider's web and an impossible puzzle and even a map of outer space.

Lucky we didn't hit that car, says Mom.

There is a knock on the door window. She tells me to roll it down.

Is the boy all right? asks a man.

He says he is, she answers.

My bones protected me, I explain, following the ridge above my eyes with a finger. They protected my brain and also my imagination.

You'll make a good football player, he says.

I'm going to be an astronaut, I reply. Spaceman Sam Winkie. This is my mom. Her name is Broadbeam—

Thanks for asking, interrupts Mom.

Another crazy Foran, I say, once we're on the street.

Have you ever really looked at your big sister? There are reasons not to. She is a Foran/Fallu, of course, with the same colour eyes and hair—Debbie's is more orange-red, like Dad's—the same freckles and nose (mine has a bump, from when I broke it at Cubs), the same bones. She also came from Mom's belly and Dad's whatever, and she also grew up at 207 Dunview Avenue. The fact is, though, she has breasts and a vagina. The fact is, she's a girl. Best not to notice things. The slingshot lying on her dresser; the panties in the basket with my underwear. The box of soft pads that I have to stand on the sink to reach (It's okay, Mom: I just tripped!); the drawings on the side of the box that make the top of my head sweaty. Best to keep away from where Grade Sevens hang out in the yard; best not to notice when she's talking to a boy after school or smoking a cigarette with her friends or, for sure, sliding down the slope into the ravine. Best to just listen as she tells Mom about her gymnastics and dancing, and they plan a Girl Guide camping weekend together. Best to thank her for helping me learn to write script and for not telling when I rode my bike through Missus Myers' flower bed. Overall, I'm proud of Debbie. Proud of my sister.

Guys fighting wars wear bandages around their heads and walk with limps. They also hit the dirt—Hit the dirt, boys!—

and crawl through the jungle on their elbows, so that the Gooks, Japs and Krauts don't hear them coming. When they reach the camp the colonel stands up and, ripping the pin from a grenade with his teeth, shouts, Let's get 'em! Spitting bullets from their machine guns, the soldiers weave around bomb craters and mangled bodies. A few poor privates hold their guts and fly backwards. Christ, they say, the bastard got lucky! The rest of the men keep firing—*rat-tat-tat-tat*—and tossing grenades. In the trenches they go hand to hand with the enemy. Using rifle butts. Plunging knives into—

Charlie!

Die, you lousy—

Pardon me?

Nothing, I say, dragging myself out of the bush. I'm not doing anything, Mom.

Could you do it a little more quietly, please? she calls from the porch. The neighbours will think there's a war over here.

Sorry.

And look at your pants!

I try wiping the grass stains off my knees, even though they look neat. Did John Glenn ever take a bath in our house? I decide to ask.

The astronaut John Glenn?

I nod.

What a remarkable question.

Thanks.

I'd better go check the dinner, says Mom. Seeing me walk a few steps, she adds: How's the limp?

Sore.

It's your other leg today.

I dive for cover behind the apple tree. Come on, men, I shout. We've still got a bridge to blow!

Blessed Trinity Church reminds me of a hockey rink. When it's full, I mean: during mass on Sunday. The room is bright, most people keep their coats on, and voices and music bounce around the high walls. Coach Byrne brought some kids from the team to a game at Maple Leaf Gardens, and afterwards I told Jimmy that whenever they played the organ during breaks, I thought of our church. Ron Ellis takes a pass from Larry Hillman in the vestibule, I said. Ellis stick-handles up the centre aisle past Father Ferguson, then slides the puck over to Frank Mahovlich. The Big M winds up twenty feet from the altar and blasts a slapshot that Father Arnot, wearing goalie pads and a silver cross, doesn't even see. Mahovlich shoots, he scores! Jimmy didn't laugh but I thought the joke was funny: Blessed Trinity Gardens, home of the Knights of Columbus Hockey League champions, 1968–69.

When it's empty, the church is a different place. I've gone over there a few times by myself. Light pours in from the tall window at the front. Some days the light is so clean I could step into it and maybe be beamed up to a spaceship. Some days the light is so dim I imagine I'm within a candle flame. The air smells of incense and wood polish. The air smells of priest. What I like best, though, is the quiet. Shut the heavy doors and Bayview Avenue goes away. So does the school: so does Willowdale. I used to think being inside the church meant I was no longer on the earth. I was floating above it, halfway to heaven. Nowadays I don't think much about heaven or God or Jesus Christ, even though he's hanging on a pole, as usual, next to the altar. Nowadays I think more about my mind being inside my body, and how the mind or the imagination—or a new word I just learned: the conscience—is impossible to touch, impossible even to locate, while the body is all touch and feeling, smell and stink. Ever located the centre of a flame? You can't.

What happened at the wedding was this. The four of us—my hippies, Missus Delmer calls us—met out front. Jill went in first. The coast is clear, she whispered through the door. We entered in single file, in case the church secretary appeared. God is *not* stupid, I prayed as I walked. He is *not* a dork. The inside door that usually shut softly clanged; the carpet that always buried the sound of shuffling feet creaked. As I neared the tabernacle—*tabernac!* I thought to myself—I scouted for hiding spots. The organ pit wasn't deep enough. The pews were too easy to see under. But a door to one confessional was open, the curtain drawn across.

Jimmy and Margaret were already waiting. They knelt before a stone altar with a small hut—the actual tabernacle—on top. In the ceiling over it was a hole always bright with white light. From the time I started going to mass, I knew the hole was a tunnel to heaven. If I looked up into it, would I see the face of Jesus? Be blinded by God's gaze? No kid had ever dared. Not even Lenny.

Come on, said Jimmy.

To act as priest, I had to stand between them and the tabernacle. That meant resting my back against the altar. Margaret gazed up at me. She had black hair and Bambi eyes. She always wore short dresses. Lately I'd started looking at her legs.

Grown-ups stay married forever, you know, I said.

Till death do us part, agreed Jimmy.

Dennis Keane's parents aren't married anymore, said Jill from behind. His dad already has another wife.

We're in love, said Margaret. She turned to Jimmy. Aren't we?

Probably, he replied.

Jill!

You said probably was good enough, answered Jill.

But I thought . . . , added Margaret, her eyes getting misty. Once he said he'd marry me . . .

Maybe we should come back— I started to say.

I *definitely* love you, okay? interrupted Jimmy.

How sweet, said Margaret.

Shh! whispered Jill. Her eyes shot over to the small door the priests sometimes used. She also crouched, as if to duck bullets. I hit the dirt, curling up underneath the altar. But Jimmy and Margaret didn't move. They kept on kneeling and kept on holding hands. From below, their faces were lit by a beautiful light, probably from the tunnel. She looked like an angel. He did too. Margaret's knees were so close I could have touched them. Her skin was as golden as, um, Kentucky Fried Chicken. She had a mole on her left thigh.

Hurry, said Jimmy. My back is getting sore.

Do you want to marry Margaret? I asked him.

I do.

Never get divorced?

Never.

Have her babies?

I guess, said Jimmy, making a face at me.

I'll have *his* babies, you mean, said Margaret.

Right.

Well . . . , said Jimmy.

Is there a ring?

Jill handed me a ring.

Cracker Jack, said Jimmy. My second try.

I always get a soldier, said Jill.

I'll trade you a ring for a soldier any day, I offered.

Hey, guys, said Margaret, smiling up at me. That did it: my legs nearly gave out and my penis started to tingle. I told Jimmy to put the ring on her finger. I told her to promise to love and cherish him.

I pronounce you man and wife, I said.

They stood, waiting again.

You may kiss the bride . . . , said Jill to me.

I don't want to, I answered, though that wasn't exactly true.

Say it to *them*.

Jimmy kissed Margaret. In front of the body and blood of Christ. Before the eyes of God. Jill and I watched. Jill didn't look at me and I didn't look at her. But I did stare at Margaret's black hair and pressed lips. I did glance at her skirt.

We kissed in the church, said Jimmy, as if just realizing it. Let's get out of here!

Big sin, agreed Jill.

They were already through the door when I turned back to the tunnel. To see up the shaft I had to place both hands on the altar—an even bigger sin, probably—and stretch. I stumbled and nearly knocked into the tabernacle. (If bits of the Eucharist spilled out, I'd go to hell for sure.) I also closed my eyes. When I opened them, would I be gazing at a smiling Jesus Christ? His frowning father? One, two, three—open! There *was* something up the hole. In the centre of the light. In the pure white. No mistaking it. No mistaking who it was, either. A rabbit. Crunching a carrot and smacking its lips. Eh, what's up, doc? said Bugs.

Have mercy on me, I prayed, racing for the exit before I bust my gut laughing. Halfway down the aisle, I noticed someone enter the church. Father Arnot? Father Ferguson? I stopped laughing. My stomach—or a spot below it—tightened. The confessional was ten feet away. Hoping it was empty, I pulled back the curtain and slipped in. The cubicle was cool and dark and smelled better than our dining room closet. I stayed in it for ages, expecting a hand to yank the curtain back and my name to be spoken. My watch had no light, but I bet I waited twenty minutes. I bet I grew older in the confessional. I bet my hair almost turned grey. Finally, my heart stopped trying to leap from my chest.

Finally, I found the courage to peek out. A woman knelt in the front pew. She was praying. Above her hung my Lord and my Saviour. His head was still bowed.

Are you a big shot, Dad?

Sorry?

A fat-cat business type?

I'm wiping my pants after messing around in the furnace room. I wasn't looking for anything in there: I was just proving that I wasn't afraid of the room anymore. (If any of my Blind River cousins visit, especially the sick girl, Elizabeth, I'll show them the furnace and ask: Want to touch it? Stick your hand inside its mouth?) Dad is on his knees measuring the sub-pump for a lid. That way, Mom won't have to lock the door anymore. That way, one of us kids won't fall in.

Definitely not, he answers.

But you wear a tie?

Lots of men wear ties. They aren't all—

Bobby Avery says you drive a fat-cat car.

He puts one hand on the sink and the other on the dryer. With a groan, Dad pulls himself up. The car originally belonged to your grandpa, he explains. We could never have afforded it ourselves.

I nod.

And being a fat-cat business type is okay, you know, he adds. I won't mind if you grow up to be one.

I'm going to be—

An astronaut, right.

Was John Glenn ever in our house? I ask.

The John Glenn?

I guess.

He just laughs.

Bathtubs can be as dangerous as spaceships, can't they? I say, the thought coming out of nowhere. They don't crash into planets or blow up in space, but you can still slip in them and crack your head.

Spaceships don't blow up, he answers. NASA would never let it happen.

Strange things happen in space *and* in bathtubs.

Okay, says Dad, laughing again. He kneels back down with a piece of plywood. I peer over his shoulder into the pump.

The Germans are down there, I warn him.

Where?

I saw their periscope the other day. It popped up in the hole, made one full turn around—all it probably saw was Mom's legs—and then popped back down.

We'd better hurry then.

In the yard it's total war. Toad—Mike, I mean—and I raid a Kraut bunker by climbing the rockery. (Mom is out shopping.) Ten-four, Sarge, says Mike as he dives for cover. What did I tell you? I shout at him. Sorry, he answers. Ten-four, Colonel Foran. We *rat-tat-tat-tat* our guns and toss grenades and mow down any Jap who tries to stop us. A Gook goes to push my brother off the cliff, but I sneak up behind and cut his throat. Bullets fly. Smoke chokes. Then Mike says, Look—a submarine spying on us from the ocean!

I race back down the rockery—the flowers are mostly dead, anyway—and plunge into the water. By the time I swim out, only the periscope is left. I grab onto it and press my eyes to the glass. Got you now, I say with an evil laugh. The periscope sinks below the surface.

Ever really look at your little brother? I'd recommend it. When boys turn five, they begin to get interesting. Begin to finally be boys. They go to kindergarten and bring back stuff in their pockets and words in their mouths. Also stories: now that he's at school, Mike has a few stories to tell, even if they're boring. (So far, he hasn't had much of a life.) He can play hide-and-seek and road hockey; he can climb the weeping willow tree and trap butterflies in his hands. Mom and Dad bought him a gerbil for his birthday and he lets me slip it under my sheets for fun. I also offer to play Dinkey cars and toy trains with him. He always says, Sure! and thinks I'm the best big brother in the world. I'm glad there are still some kid toys left in the house. I'm glad, I guess, we still share a room. (If he touches my hockey cards, he dies.) Mom and Dad are sure lucky we sleep together. When he hears monsters under his bed, I'm there to check. When he's too scared to get up and pee, I open the closet door and say, See, Mike, it's empty. Next year, when he starts to learn letters, I'll help him with the hard ones—G and K, Q and W. When he gets interested in books without pictures, I'll read him my favourites. He writes with his right hand and his hair is sandy blond. Otherwise, he's all Foran/Fallu: the mouth and eyes, the nose and cheekbones. (Bones, bones!) He's a good kid, Mike. I'm proud of the boy.

What happened in the ravine was this. Jimmy passed me a note one afternoon that said he and Margaret were going on their honeymoon after school. Jill saw me read it and looked excited. Jimmy noticed, and he had Matt Kelly send another note that said: NOT JILL. I thought that was mean—now that Brenda Deane had stopped chasing me and Joanne Kuri wasn't talking to Jimmy, Jill was the fourth in our group, and she was great, though I never thought about kissing her—and for the rest of the afternoon I pretended to be working on an answer. Jimmy kept looking over. Twice Missus Delmer asked him to watch the board, not his friend. But I wasn't writing him a note. I was just doodling. Faces and animals. Lines that connected like smashed windshields. I also tried to draw galaxies. Space used to look normal: the sun in the centre with the nine planets, plus their moons, circling around it. Then I read a *National Geographic* that showed photos of things that looked like paintings by kindergarten kids, but were actually galaxies and solar systems. The article said these galaxies were way bigger than our own. Way more moons and way larger planets and suns so enormous and boiling a spaceship would fry if it got near. Where were these solar systems located? Beyond ours. Beyond, in a way, our imaginations. In a place—a new place—called deep space.

Your first time? asked Jimmy, as we slipped into the tall grass behind the church.

You know it is.

Don't worry, said Margaret. Jimmy has been down there before.

If my sister sees me . . .

Grade Sevens and Eights are at the museum today, he said. I checked.

Incredible how small the culvert was. Amazing how shallow the stream. I guess I wanted the stream to be a roaring river and the culvert a tunnel. I guess I wanted to be balancing on a rock in the river and suddenly hear the *whoo-whoo*. Maybe I wanted to gaze into the tunnel and watch a headlight punch a hole in the black. To stand there as the train shot out.

Sunlight made the water sparkle. Sunlight also lit up the culvert. Using stones dropped by kids, we walked right in without soaking our feet. I said H-E-L-L-O but my voice sounded less like God's than it did in the bath. I studied the walls and found only a few so-and-so LOVES so-and-sos and a drawing of a boy with a penis coming out of his pants. Just studying the drawing sent blood into my face. Soggy cigarettes spotted the stones. Shrivelled balloons stuck to the curved walls.

Jimmy and Margaret kissed. More than kissed: they started necking. She pressed against him. He ate her lips. She wore a sweater and a short dress. The top button of his shirt was done up. (He usually did it up only for mass.) I watched them for a while, especially her legs, but then I began to worry that my own penis was going to act like the boy's in the drawing. Was I ever sweaty. Was my heart ever thumping. Gazing deeper into the tunnel helped calm me—it—down. So did mumbling an Our Father. When Jimmy and Margaret finally separated, they were both purple-red. She stared at his pants and giggled. He stared and giggled too.

Want to kiss her? asked Jimmy.

What?

She doesn't mind.

Come here, said Margaret.

I thought about it for a second. Then I changed rocks with Jimmy. Margaret took some lip gloss from her pocket and did a quick rub. Ready? she asked.

I couldn't speak.

She put her left hand on my shoulder. I did the same, almost knocking us into the water. Put your hand around my waist, silly, she said.

Her face was inches from mine. Her blue eyes and cute nose, her glossy lips. Then her eyelids dropped. Then she made her mouth pouty.

Don't tell Brenda, I managed.

We kissed.

Not for too long, I heard Jimmy say.

It happened immediately. Not the electricity running through my body. Not the prickly sensation. The bulge. The bulge in my pants.

Don't bother to hide it, said Jimmy.

It's cute, added Margaret.

I have to go, I said, stepping into the stream with both feet.

Smart, said Jimmy.

Two soakers, I groaned. My mom will know!

I scrambled up the wall to the bottom of the slope. Jimmy followed. Before climbing over the railing onto the sidewalk, I checked my pants.

You can't tell afterwards, he said. That's the great part.

We walked up Finch, my shoes going squish.

Felt great, eh?

Was that first base? I asked.

At least first, he answered. I hope Margaret doesn't get pregnant.

A chill spread over my body. We'd be the dad! I said, checking to make sure no one was near.

Jimmy stopped. *Charlie and Margaret sitting in a tree*, he said. *K-I-S-S-I-N-G*.

Quit it.

First comes love, then comes marriage—

Jimmy . . .

Then comes the baby in the baby carriage!

Even after the Blue Fairy brought Pinocchio to life, he was still just a body. A body made of wood. Wood shaped into bones. Having a body meant he was alive but not awake. To be awake, Pinocchio had to find a conscience. That was a small voice inside his head that would help him tell right from wrong. Be a guide on the path. Warn against temptation. The Blue Fairy couldn't do it, so she asked Jiminy Cricket. She told Jiminy to kneel and tapped him on each shoulder with a wand. *Poof,* suddenly he had new clothes. *Poof,* suddenly he was Sir Jiminy Cricket and his job was to act as Pinocchio's conscience. Be a good boy, said the Blue Fairy to Pinocchio. And remember to always let your conscience be your guide.

Winter is over but the metal is still cold. Hard as bone: ready to bruise. Broken glass twinkles around the base. A girl's slingshot hangs off the tail. I step up into the rocket part and climb towards the tip. The best way into the globe is between the bars. Step across open air. Walk in space. Six-year-olds hang upside down in the globe. Eight-year-olds fight each other. Nine-and-a-half-year-old boys usually don't bother. I hunch my shoulders and let my feet dangle. If the rocket is the body, the globe must be the head. And the head, I now know, is where all the important but hard to understand stuff goes on.

Apollo Thirteen is still lost in space this morning. (Is the space deep?) Dad thinks the ship may not make it back. Mom says a prayer for the men. The whole world is watching, announces the man on TV, but he must mean it in a symbol way, like saying that God is watching us all. Down on earth, we can't see the Apollo twirling and spinning and maybe getting ready to blow up. We can only imagine it. Imagine the astronauts inside the ship and the thoughts inside the astronauts. That's what I'm doing. Squished in the globe with my legs flopping. Gazing up at a blue sky of clouds drifting slowly by.

1970

September

Bless me, Father, for I have sinned. It has been twelve weeks since my last—

Twelve weeks? You didn't go during the summer?

We were on vacation.

Where?

Blind River.

Don't they have churches in Blind River?

Lots of them, I answer, shifting on the kneeler. My mom took us to mass every Sunday, even though it was in French.

Did they offer confession only in French?

I don't know. I mean, probably. But most people speak both languages.

Mmm. Go on, son.

The *mmm* is a giveaway: it's Father Arnot today. He isn't as scary as Father Ferguson and gives easier penance, but he's also boring. He never seems interested: he never wants to chat. Knowing who you're confessing to is important. What to tell. What to hide. How often to lie. How big the lies should be. Knowing who the priest is also makes me less nervous. Jimmy says they want us nervous in the confessional. They want us on our knees in the dark, staring at a shut window, waiting. Our hearts fluttering. Our ears hearing murmurs and coughs. They—the priests and nuns, the Pope and God—want us to jump out of our skins when the wood is finally slid back, *whack,* and the thousands of holes in the screen filter pencils of light.

. . . since my last confession. Since then I have . . . hit my brother and disobeyed my mother. Also, I, um, I looked in my sister's underwear drawer, though I didn't find much. Also, I dropped our cat Tigger into the toilet. Just to see what she'd do.

And?

She tried to climb back out. But her nails—

I'm not interested in your cat, child.

You're not?

Have you anything else to tell me about?

You want more sins?

It isn't what I want. Are you sure you've told God everything on your conscience? Everything from the last three months?

Oh, I say. Well, I, um, I . . . Oh yeah. I . . .

DARED MIKE TO EAT DOG SHIT? LET MY PENIS GET HARD THINKING ABOUT A BRA? WISHED THAT MY COUSIN ELIZABETH, DOWN IN TORONTO TO VISIT SOME DOCTORS, WOULD GET BETTER, SO SHE'D STOP

SLEEPING IN OUR BASEMENT? STABBED A CATFISH IN *TANTE* MARIE'S SINK AND WATCHED IT OOZE BLOOD? LIED TO MY DAD ABOUT HOW MUCH WORK I DID ON KEITH HEALY'S TREE FORT?

I forgot to make my bed, I finally answer. Two days in a row. My mom said she was disappointed.

Mmm, says Father Arnot. (Father Ferguson would be groaning by now.) And?

For these and all my sins, I am truly sorry.

Say four Our Fathers, three Hail Marys and one Glory Be for the sins you've committed but can't seem to recall.

Is it bad that I can't remember more?

That's not for me to comment on. Only you—and the Lord—know your heart.

I know my heart?

If not you, then who?

Oh.

You'll do better next month, I'm sure, he says. There is a silence. Go ahead, he adds.

O my God, I am heartily sorry for having offended thee, and I detest my sins above every other evil, because—

He raises his right hand—you can see it through the screen—and cuts me off with the mumble. *God, the father of mercy, reconciled . . . mumblemumble . . . May he grant you pardon . . . mumblemumble . . . I absolve you from your sins in the name of the Father, and of the Son, and of the Holy Spirit.*

Amen, I say, and bless myself.

Go in peace.

Thanks, Father. I rise to one knee. With Father Arnot,

it's usually a waste of time to start a conversation. He used the word, though. He brought it up. Could I ask you something? I say.

He is silent.

What's a stream of conscience?

Sorry?

I read it in a book.

Never heard of such a thing.

Does our conscience move like water in a—

Ask your teacher, he interrupts. I've twenty more children to see.

I rise from the kneeler, hear the click that shuts off the red bulb above the confessional and pull back the curtain. Most kids return to the pew where their friends are and try saying penance with jokes in their ears and pokes in their ribs. I like the short pews near the tabernacle. They're always empty. Light from the windows is lemony. Light from the tunnel-to-heaven is milk frozen in mid-air. I smell incense and candles, a nice mix. Church sounds go quiet: the sea returns.

I first heard the sea last summer. The same day that I earned my Senior, the highest a kid can reach at ten, I came home from the pool with the ocean in my ears. No crashing waves or howling wind. Just water over a shore and a steady breeze. A seashell sound. An almost echo. I've got the ocean in my head, Mom, I said with a laugh. The ocean in your head, she answered, and your cousin Elizabeth downstairs. The poor girl isn't well, added Mom. I'd love it if you and Debbie spent some time with her. Sure, I said, though to be honest I'd rather have played with Elizabeth in Blind River, where she belonged. Anyway, the next morning I was too sick to even think about my cousin. My left ear had swollen shut. One side of my face was a double bee sting. I couldn't eat. I could barely stand. (When I peed, I missed the bowl.) All I could do was lie quiet and still, listen to crows on the telephone wires and cars in the street and the *hmmm* of the 401. After a few minutes or hours of not moving, I began to hear my eyelashes beat and feel my body breathe. If I closed my eyes, I floated up above myself and gazed back down at the sick boy in bed. If I closed my eyes, I left me behind. Had I shut them for longer, I bet I would have drifted down the stairs, through the dining room and kitchen, then down another staircase to the basement. To see who was there. To ask what they wanted. But I was scared enough as it was. Once, the throb got so bad I jammed a finger into the eardrum. It was like a rug shock, except a thousand times stronger, and I crashed to the floor. When I woke up, vomit was gushing from my mouth and nose. That's when I understood: the ache wasn't anything I could scrape out with a finger or blow out with a tissue. The infection had gone too far in. Only medicine and rest could fix it.

Hi-ho, hi-ho, sang the Red Dwarfs who marched into my ear all day. They carried shovels and picks and none of them returned. *Where are you going with those tools?* I wanted to ask. Only, I couldn't talk. My mouth was gagged. My arms and legs were tied to the ground with ropes. (Mom brought some library books home. After a few pages of reading, I grew dizzy.) *It's off to work we go!*

I missed a week at the tree fort. The Healys' backyard joins the Campbells', and Keith and George decided to build a fort near the fence. Keith was on the job day and night, sometimes with a flashlight. He drew designs. He kept a pencil behind his ear and nails between his lips. George was excellent at hammering and sawing and following Keith's instructions. His mom brought out Kool-Aid and sandwiches. I could hold boards to be sawed, though I always worried about losing a finger, and I didn't mind hammering extra nails into floors and walls, so long as they were already secure. My dad supplied most of the wood and nails and just about any tool Keith wanted. The minute he returned home from work—between six fifteen and six thirty most nights, though I'd stopped showing off that I could tell time—he'd ask about the fort. How was the new roof coming? Did those cement blocks help secure the foundation? Was I going back after supper, and could he tag along for a look? No question, Dad felt worse about the sick week than I did. He bought me a set of screwdrivers. He painted the words BIG SAM on my construction helmet, without asking first.

What I missed about the tree fort was sitting quietly on the top floor until a bird landed. I missed watching sunlight through branches and insects on leaves. I missed surprising squirrels who weren't expecting to see a boy up there; I missed feeling the rain before it hit the earth. What I also missed about the tree fort was how it made me think nice thoughts about my cousin Elizabeth. High above the ground, cool in the shade, I could finally feel sorry for the girl stuck in our basement with nothing to do but read magazines and watch TV, wait for someone to drive her to the hospital. (For tests and more tests, said Mom. To figure out why she's so small, said Dad. To make sure she doesn't die, said Debbie.) The rec room couch was lumpy. The air kept clothes damp. The only window, above her head, showed our driveway. Even if Elizabeth stood on her tippy-toes, her nightgown stretched to her knees, all she could see was a parked car or empty pavement. No one skipped or played hopscotch out there anymore. A tree blocked the sun.

That was the summer. Up the tree fort ladder and down the basement stairs; dwarfs mining my head and Timothy-the-turtle mining the rockery. Waves on a beach. Seashell echoes. That was the summer, half before I turned ten, half after. The end. The beginning. Miss Ford, Grade 5a, Room 10. Miss Ford and the mystery balloon. My secret church friend. My Jiminy Cricket. Watch for it. Watch for it in the tunnel-to-heaven. The string will descend the hole and curl on the altar like a snake, followed by the incredible ball, so round it could be the sun, so red it could be my beating heart; then the balloon will shift sideways until the low roof ends and it can sail away to the wide open sky. The sky of the ceiling. The ceiling of the church.

Watch for it.

Diary of a Cat (Part 1)

Hi. My name is Pascal and I'm a cat. "Wow," is that fun. You sleep in the sun and lic yourself clean and chase birds you don't realy want to eat. Nice people make you talk with an accent: purrr. Bad kids pull your tale.

Most cats live with familys. Tigger the black and orange cat lives with the Forans. They're great. They eat pik—picknics in their yard. One day I come in. "Hey," says a nice boy named Charlie, "look at that grey cat." His nice dad says, "Come hear, kittie." He picks me up, wow. He scratches my neck and ears. I purr. "What do you know," says the dad. "He's a droolur!" "He's dirty," says the mom, who is still nice. "Put him down, Dave."

The mom gives me some chicken. It's delis—delishus. I eat it all, then lic myself. The nice Dad picks me up again. Purrr, I say to him. "That's disgusting," says the big sister, who is a moodie teen-age-r. "Lets call him Droolur," says the dad. "Find a rag, will you, Moo?"

All cats need a family for food and a place to sleep. The Forans are great. I'll live with them.

"Bye for now."

December

Bless me, Father, for I have sinned. It has been—

Let me guess. Four weeks? Since last first Friday mass?

Hi, Father Ferguson.

Pay less attention to who I am, son, and more to your own sinning self.

Sorry.

Start over, he says, blowing air from his cheeks. He also

jiggles his jowls. Slivers of light, bouncing off his glasses, shoot through the holes.

Bless me, Father, for I have sinned. It has been four weeks since my last confession. Since then I have . . . done lots of bad stuff.

He snorts—his way of laughing. Tell me the thoughts in your heart, he says.

Want my stream of conscience?

Eh? Fine.

Okay, I say, excited by my list. (For once, there's a real sin I'm willing to talk about.) I got into a fight with another boy, Father. That was wrong. I know it was. He started it, or maybe I did, but pretty soon we were fighting hard.

Did you want to hurt this boy?

I guess so.

Have you made up since?

Kind of.

Would you like to?

His dad is our hockey coach.

That isn't—

He's my friend.

Go on.

Other sins?

Some more stream of conscience, perhaps, he says with another snort.

Is he making fun of me? Though my nose almost touches the screen, I still can't see much. Up close, though, I smell an adult. I figured the scent would be like my dad:

cigarettes and Old Spice, freckled oranges. Instead, I smell Grandma Ruthie. Her medicine. Her oldness.

Let me think . . . I say. (I thought the fight would be enough!) THAT I MESS WITH MY PENIS MOST DAYS, SOMETIMES UNTIL GUNK SHOOTS OUT? THAT I TOLD EVERYONE I SHOULD BE NAMED CUB OF THE YEAR, EVEN THOUGH JIMMY HAS AS MANY STARS AND BADGES? THAT I BARELY SAID HELLO TO MY COUSIN ELIZABETH WHEN SHE STAYED ANOTHER WEEK IN OUR BASEMENT IN OCTOBER? THAT I PRETENDED TO STUFF BODIES IN CAR TRUNKS, AS PART OF A GAME THAT KEITH HEALY CALLED F-L-Q? THAT I LIED TO JIMMY ABOUT BEING UPSET WHEN COACH BYRNE PUT ME IN MORE GAMES? THAT I PRETENDED NOT TO SEE THE WORDS WRITTEN ON THE CLASSROOM BOARD THAT FINALLY DROVE NELLIE PARKER OFF THE DEEP END?

I spit a lot, I say. We call it hawking. And I used a bad word the other day. I said—

Details aren't necessary.

Okay.

He sighs. His breath nearly knocks me off the kneeler.

The parts do not add up to the whole, it seems, he says.

Father?

Given what goes on in that schoolyard, and what we are told about behaviour towards teachers, never mind the smoking and drinking and premature sexual activity in the ravine behind this very building; given all that, God should be privy to more truthful, more *ardently* truthful confessions of errors and wrongdoings.

Sorry, I repeat.

But then we believe the devil vanquished, don't we?

I say nothing.

The devil vanquished and God triumphant. Triumphant and alone. No opposite. No balance. The end of the old thinking. The beginning of the new. How wrong we are about that. How terribly wrong.

Chatting with Father Ferguson is good; having to listen to him give a sermon, especially when he uses words I don't know, makes me squirm. My knees are aching and my back is getting sore. I'd love to rest my bum on my heels.

Forget what I just said, he adds. Murky puddles of thought. Nothing more. *For these and . . .* , he begins.

For these and all my sins, I am heartily sorry.

For contrition, I'd like you to say three Hail Marys and an Our Father.

That's all?

Plus a Glory Be, for my soul.

Yours?

Don't ask questions.

Father Ferguson raises his hand. Do your part, he says, and I'll do mine. *O my God . . .* , I say. *God, the father of mercy . . .* , he says. *I detest my sins above every other . . .* , I say. *Ministry of the Church . . .* , he says. *Because they displease Thee, my God . . .* , I say, hoping he hurries up (I can never remember the final lines). *And I absolve you from all your sins, in the name of the Father, and of the Son, and of the Holy Spirit.*

Amen, we say together.

Go in peace.

Thanks.

And don't forget.

About the devil?

Another snort. The prayer for me, he answers.

Glory be to the Father, I murmur in a pew near the tabernacle, *and to the Son, and to the Holy Spirit, as it was in the beginning and ever shall be, world without end, Amen.* I've never prayed for a priest before. At least it's honest penance, though. Most of my confession was a puddle. A deep, murky puddle hidden by a curb. The kind you don't notice until it's too late. The kind you step in wearing good shoes—new Adidas, say—and come out splattered and soaked.

Lying is easy when it's just forgetting to mention certain things. Like my fight with Tim Byrne. It was actually the end of a long story. To begin, I have to go back to the first day of school in September and talk about Adidas Rom. White skin and laces, three blue stripes. Tim was wearing them that morning. So were Matt Kelly and Lucci Pavese—his father is a dentist—and Greg Simic. I had on my old canvas shoes. But Mom said I certainly needed new runners, and she'd been chatting with Missus Byrne, who told her that Adidas Rom were the best. At Northtown Shopping Centre, she saw the price—twenty-five dollars, no discount—and asked the man, For boys' running shoes? He shrugged: Mom wrote a cheque. I wore them the next day. Jimmy's face fell when he saw me. *Boom:* I can tell right away when he is hurt. (We've been friends since kindergarten, which I hardly remember.) His birthday was near the end of the month, and for sure he was going to get Adidas Rom as well. You *do* run faster in them, I mentioned. When I get mine, he replied, I'll run faster than you! (That was weird: he already did.) I was hoping he might have a birthday party. The next Monday, however, I caught up to him above the ravine. He was wearing his church shoes. Where are your—? I started to say. In here, he replied, opening his knapsack. His face told me (again) what he was feeling. In his knapsack was a pair of Adidas Gym, red skin and laces with black stripes (sixteen dollars). They're still cool, I told him. No they're not, he answered. Better than your church shoes, I said. Jimmy disagreed. I can't wear Adidas Gym, he replied. Everyone will laugh at me.

They won't even notice, I said.

Was I wrong. Wrong about how the guys would react to his runners—*Look at Reilly's fairy shoes!*—and wrong about Jimmy's threat to throw them into the ravine after school. I slid down the slope to catch the Adidas Gym before they landed in the stream. Scrapes on my arms, burrs stuck to my pants and socks: I didn't care, so long as I saved the shoes. By the time I climbed back out, Jimmy was two blocks farther along Finch, even though he wore only socks. I caught up. Put them on, I panted. Please. See how fast you ran in your Adidas Rom? he said, his eyes pools—not puddles—of water. See?

Then came the hockey mess. That's what it was (and still is): a murky, muddy mess. My parents are friends with Coach and Missus Byrne. I'm friends with their oldest son, Tim, except when we fight. The Byrne house has a bar in the basement and an in-ground pool out back. Tim gets a huge room to himself. Before the season started, Coach Byrne helped Dad buy some equipment for me, at a special coaches-only discount. I got new pads and a new blocker and glove. I also got two goalie sticks: Sherwood, the best. I let Jimmy borrow a stick for practices. I also said he could use my catcher during games, if he wanted. Until this season, we split the games. One of us started, the other finished. In October, the coach decided we should play a full game each, and rotate. I said okay. Jimmy told me he bet that Coach Byrne would put me in more often. (Remember last season? he said. Remember when we played St. Gabriel's?) He wants you to be the number one goalie, he added. I'm just the back-up. Not a chance, I answered. We're partners.

Was I wrong.

I played three games in a row. We lost the third one nine to four, and I stunk. Two goals went between my legs. Two more I scored on myself. Jimmy was in the car with us afterwards and he refused to talk to me or Dad. (Some of those boys look as if they shave! said Dad about the other team.) The next day he told me he was quitting. That's stupid, I answered. You don't know it will always be this way. Yes I do, he said. How can you? I asked. Jimmy shrugged. You wouldn't understand, he replied, and walked off (in his Adidas Gym).

That's when—and maybe why—I fought Tim Byrne. Tim never said I stunk. He never said I cost us the game. We just started to argue about who was better, Dave Keon or Jean Beliveau, and then Tim said that tripping was okay in British

Bulldog and I said it was cheating. We were both talking low and hard and we were both glaring. Want to fight about it? he finally asked. If you do, I answered. If *you* do, he replied.

I shoved him. Okay, he said, getting up. I was expecting the super-fast punch that Lenny Grusa throws, before the other boy even knows what is happening. What Tim did was drop to his knees and grab my ankles. All of a sudden my feet were in the air; all of a sudden I was on my rear. I charged. Again he dropped down low, letting me pummel his ribs, and *wham*, I was back where I started. Kids formed a circle around us. Stop it, guys! said Jill. Matt shouted, Punch him, Charlie! Lenny walked into the middle of the fight, shook his head and said: If he did that to me, I'd scratch his eyes out. Three more times Tim did it to me. Three more times I wound up on my ass. Finally, he slid onto my chest and pinned me down. Give up? he said with a strange grin. I guess, I answered. Say it, he ordered. So everyone can hear you. Some kids, like Jill and Matt, had already left; others still stood there. Where was Jimmy? I suddenly wondered. I give up, I finally said. Louder, said Tim. I GIVE UP.

I told you to scratch his eyes out, said Lenny afterwards. One of the Macmillan boys called me a spaz. You should have kicked him in the balls, he added.

Next day I sent Mike downstairs with a message. Mom came up and asked if I honestly was sick. My ear, I answered, making a head sandwich with the pillow. It's worse than last summer. (Liar!) She let me watch TV until lunch: *The Friendly Giant* and *Mr. Dress-Up*, *The Price Is Right* and *Hollywood Squares*. In the afternoon I read *The Red Balloon* for maybe the fifteenth time. A boy named Pascal lives in Paris with his mother. She is old and has a moustache. (The book includes photos.) He has no dad. One day Pascal finds a red balloon hanging on a lamppost. He pulls it loose and, amazing, the balloon follows him. People try to separate the boy from his discovery—the school principal and his mom, neighbourhood bullies in short pants (*pantalons courts*, we learned in French class: *Henri Leduc porte des pantalons courts*)—but it stays by his side. They become friends. The balloon becomes part of him. Then a terrible thing happens: the bullies chase Pascal through the streets of Paris and beat him up. (I'm not a bullie, Nellie, I'll say to her when we finally talk. I'm not like those kids. Sticks and stones may break my bones, she might answer. But words will—Will you remember? I'll interrupt. What, she will probably reply, remember that all the kids at Blessed Trinity were cruel to me? I wasn't that way, I'll answer in a panic. You have to remember *me* differently . . .) The bullies also toss rocks at the balloon. It bursts. The air goes out and the skin shrivels, the way it does on old people. Pascal is devastated. That part of him shrivels too. That part of him dies.

Spend some time with the girl, said Mom when Elizabeth stayed with us again after Thanksgiving. Tell her about your day. Okay, okay, I answered, so she'd quit staring at me. Two steps down into the basement, I stopped and sat. Hi, said my Blind River cousin, black-haired and cow-eyed in her nightgown. Hi, I replied. The TV was on. The curtain was closed. A blanket covered her legs. A stuffed animal—a bunny, maybe—showed from under a cushion. Seeing me notice it, Elizabeth pushed the bunny back out of sight. Good TV in Toronto, eh? she said. Lots more channels. *Tur-on-uh?* I thought to myself. It's okay, I answered. Nothing on most of the time. Yeah, said my cousin. I looked around some more: at the carpet, at the walls, at the rows of *National Geographic*s above Mom's sewing table. You coming all the way down, Charlie? she asked, witch-haired and bug-eyed in her cloak. Can't, I said, standing up. I have a hockey game. When she smiled, her face suddenly looked a lot like her mom's—my *tante* Carole, who was fine—but also a little like *my* mom's, who honestly wasn't sick. You a goalie, eh? said Elizabeth. She used that word too much—eh. Like youz and geez. Like *câlice!* and *tabernac!* We're the best team in the league, I replied. She smiled again, for no reason. I'd love to watch you play sometime, she said. I took a step. What could I say? *We don't play in basements? You don't really live in Tor-on-to?* Sure, I answered. I'll ask my mom if it's okay. Thanks, said my cousin. You and Debbie and Mike are the best.

But then Pascal looks up. What does he see? Not one balloon. Not five. Twenty-three! Of all colours, their strings tied into a rope. The boy rushes to the spot. He grabs the rope and is lifted high, high into the sky.

Where children don't cry. High in the sky. Where children aren't sick. High in the sky. *Spend some time with the girl. Tell her about your—* My day in my head? My time in the base-ment? How could they write those terrible things? *You wouldn't understand.* Gym is Jim and Jimmy is Jiminy. Rom is just Rom. *Okay, okay,* I answered and sat partway down. *Hi,* she said, black-haired and bug-eyed in her gown. *Suzette Leduc porte une robe de chambre.* (I hear her sobs at night.) *You still quit?* I said to him, meaning to say *sick*. (It's just not right.) Nellie Parker's eyes are grey. (I don't know what to say.) Tell her about your— (It wasn't me who made her that way!) Sticks and stones won't break my bones but words will surely—

But then he looks up. What does he see? Dropping down the tunnel, its string dangling? Floating out to where the low ceiling stops? The red balloon, reaching the open air. The red balloon, soon to be free.

Diary of a Cat (Part 2)

Hi, it's me again. Pascal the purring cat. Still a grey kittie with no home. Still getting fed by the nice Foran family. The dad, who calls me Droolur, carved a bucket and tried to tye it around my neck. A drool bucket, "ha ha." The nice son, Charlie, pets me until I talk with my accent. He's my best friend. Their other cat, Tigger, is mean.

Sleeping outside is no fun now. Pretty soon I'll need a warm place at night. I meow and meow on the porch until the nice mom opens the door. I eat all the food in Tiggers dish, eat it fast, making drool. The mom says that's okay and my long hair is okay and even my smell is okay. But not my spray. "Wow," I shoot a sticky spray out my pee hole. "Wow," I shoot it on tables and chairs and even the dad's pants. They get angry. "He cant come in anymore if he does that," says the mom.

"Stop spraying, Pascal," says Charlie into my ear. "Please stop!"

I sure better, eh? Winter is coming. No way a poor animal can survive outside.

March

Bless me, Father, for I have sinned. It has been four weeks since my last confession. Since then I— Since then— I sneeze.

Bless you indeed, says the priest.

There's a smell . . .

His laugh nearly blows the curtain open. His laugh is a hurricane and his breath is a peppermint and he's wearing enough cologne to drown a kid in his own jacket. He's Father Larry, new to the priesthood and new to Blessed Trinity. With us for a short while, announced Father Ferguson at mass.

I forget how stuffy it gets in these things, he tells me. Beginner's mistake.

Like being in the trunk of a car, I say.

Not that bad!

Sorry, Father.

Don't be, he answers. I threw us off track . . . *four weeks since my last . . .*

. . . *confession,* I say. *Since then I have . . .* the usual stuff, I guess. Spitting and swearing and not always being nice to my brother. Also, even though I was named Cub of the Year in January I still didn't have the hobby badge. All the other kids in the Super Six have it.

The Super Six?

It's a special six with the best cubs in the pack, I explain. They decided to put us together, to set an example. Just like Miss Ford did.

Your teacher?

She divided the class into three rows. The window row, where I sit, is the Supersmart group. The middle row is the Smart group. The row near the door is the Dumb—

Did Miss Ford use these names?

She didn't call the rows anything. You knew right away, though, by who got put where.

The priest makes a sound. It isn't Father Ferguson's *gur* or Father Arnot's *tch*. The sound is more a *whew*, young and strong. You were telling me about Cubs, he says.

I'm no good at crafts, I answer. My dad is amazing, though, and he carved a Roman chariot on a stand. I painted the chariot and brought it in.

Did you say you'd made it yourself?

No one asked.

But were you still telling a lie?

I didn't tell anyone anything, I reply. I didn't lie: I just acted dishonest.

He laughs again. Touché, he says. Is there any school stuff you'd like to talk to God about?

I hesitate.

I've been hearing from the other priests and teachers about some troubles, he adds. Smoking and drinking. Unkind behaviour towards certain students.

You mean Nellie Parker?

I don't know names yet.

Kids treat her terribly, I say, even though she's just ill and lonely and also maybe a little homesick. Once, they wrote these words on the—

My fault, he interrupts. You don't need to—

What they said about her was evil, I finish, getting a thought off my mind.

Father Larry is quiet. I watch him through the screen. His hair is a toothbrush, his eyes are Bobby Hull blue. His teeth are whiter than his collar. His jaw is huge. When he talks, his neck puffs. When he hands out the host at mass, muscles slither in his arm.

God is the god of light, he finally says. We are all his children. You, me *and* the kids who wrote those words about that girl. God knows we sin. He knows we are flawed. But that does not mean we are dirty or stained. To be baptized is to be cleansed. To confess is to be born again.

I almost ask him a question: if eating the apple meant the end of Eden but the beginning of us, was it so bad? Wasn't the devil, disguised as a snake, helping out? Helping make us who we are—Sons of Adam, Daughters of Eve? I used to see God's light in my bedroom, I answer instead. The beam poured through the window. I'd sit in it for ages, feeling warm and happy.

Cool.

I was just a kid.

Why should it be different now?

I don't know how to reply. Do children ever die? I ask him.

Sometimes.

Even if they sit in the light?

Know what? says Father Larry. You seem like a nice boy. God is happy to forgive your sins. Go sit by yourself for a while and think about the hobby badge, and any other things we didn't have a chance to chat about today.

You mean other sins?

Other things, he corrects.

MORE SPEWING PENIS STUFF? MORE TOUCHING MY SISTER'S UNDERWEAR AND STEALING A TAMPAX FROM THE CUPBOARD TO STUDY IT? MORE TRICKING GRADE THREES OUT OF THEIR BEST HOCKEY CARDS: GARY SMITH AND VIC HADFIELD FOR THE MAHOVLICH BROTHERS? OR WHAT I SAID TO JIMMY WHEN HE TOLD ME I DIDN'T DESERVE THE HOBBY BADGE, EVEN THOUGH HE WAS RIGHT? OR HOW I'VE BEGUN TO PICK AT THE SKIN AROUND MY THUMBNAILS UNTIL THEY BLEED?

For these and all my sins, I say, *I am heartily sorry.*

I know you are, he says. Don't bother with contrition. I'll just whiz through my lines.

The other priests mumble them.

I bet they do, he replies. He raises his hand. *God the father of . . . so on and so forth . . . in abundance for the forgiveness . . . so on and so forth . . . ministry of the Church. And I absolve you from your sins in the name of the Father, and of the Son, and of the Holy Spirit.*

Amen.

Go in peace, son, he says. And stay cool.

Far out, I answer, because Debbie says it.

He laughs again.

Click, the light goes off. *Click*, my uneasiness slips away. Walking up the aisle I hum a song from the new folk mass, which Mom takes us to now: *A new day / A new day is on its way / With one heart and one song / For ehh-verrr*. Shh, says Miss Ford. I smile at her and genuflect next to a pew swimming in window light. Sitting in the light *is* like being a kid by his bedroom window, I decide. Feeling warm and happy. Not worrying about dumb ideas. At last I realize what is so weird: the priest didn't assign me penance! Just think for a bit, said Father Larry.

No problem, Father.

Our class did a thinking exercise last week. We were told to get our coats and boots on for a special meeting at the church. In the hall we met Father Murray, who had come all the way from downtown to work with us. He was a tall man in a priest suit that was half pants, half dress. He had a shaved head and a silver crucifix. His brows hid the colour of his eyes. Listen to me, boys and girls, said Father Murray in a soldier's voice. Listen closely.

Do any of you know what a nuclear holocaust is? he asked. It's a war waged using weapons of mass destruction. A bomb that can wipe out an entire city, such as Willowdale or even all Toronto. A bomb that does so much damage, survivors of the attack will need to start over, rebuild society. Today, I want us to think about how that might happen. Let's say there is a shelter under this church that is big enough for twenty people. Which citizens would you want saved? Don't name names: only professions. Should you have a doctor in the shelter? A lawyer or a banker? Each group can choose twenty types. No fewer and no more. Remember that these bombs exist, children; they've already been used. This is a serious, adult task. Go to work, added Father Murray. There isn't time to waste.

My group had three boys and three girls. No one wanted to speak first. But then Lucci got us started by saying that, of course, we needed a dentist on our list. Greg Simic, whose father fixes people's backs, said a doctor for people with bad backs was important. Suzy Garner, whose dad owns a camera store, said a photographer was an obvious choice; Gina Giordani, whose father once did some work for mine, said we better have a contractor to build new houses. I wanted to mention how important shopping malls were, but the choices made me so annoyed that I chose something dumb: Hockey player. Bobby Orr or Jean Beliveau. John Sealy, who can be a suck, said we'd better include a priest.

Father Murray asked for the sheets of paper. He wrote the jobs on a blackboard, putting check marks beside those selected by more than one group. Lawyer, doctor and priest all got four checks. Nurse and teacher received three: the Queen and Pope made only two lists. (We forgot about them.) Hockey player also got two votes, and I was disappointed that someone else thought of book writer. Once the professions were on the board, the priest started to criticize them. First, bricklayer. Who chose this? he asked. Joe Motolla, whose dad reminds me of Mister Giano back in Grade Three, raised his hand. Stand, said Father Murray. Joe glanced over at Miss Ford, who sat in a chair with her arms crossed. She nodded to him. Then the priest asked about bus driver. Who chose—? he began to say. Before he could finish, Jimmy shot up. You need someone to drive buses, don't you? he said. Of course, answered the priest. Both you boys have listed good jobs. But are they essential to this new world? A lawyer could lay bricks for a building. A doctor could drive a bus. But would either of you want a bus driver to deliver your wife's baby? A bricklayer to create a system of laws?

A line of red climbed Joe Motolla's neck to his cheeks. He sank back to the floor. Jimmy also blushed and squeezed his hands into fists. But he stayed on his feet and repeated: You still need someone to drive the bus.

I've explained that already, son, said Father Murray, his smile false. (It's easy to tell with grown-ups.) And don't get sharp with me. What we are doing is too urgent to waste time on one stubborn boy. All work is important. But the job you chose is BLUE collar, not WHITE. It doesn't require education. It isn't skilled. The priest picked up the brush. Those are non-essential jobs, he added, erasing bus driver and bricklayer, photographer and book writer, hockey player and ballerina.

I found Jimmy in the senior washroom later that day. Guys were whipping globs of wet toilet paper, but he stood looking out the window. I didn't choose my own dad's job, I said to make him feel better. I didn't choose shopping mall supervisor. What's wrong with choosing your own dad's job? he answered. Nothing, I said quickly. I didn't mean it that way. Yes you did, he said. Want to come to my house after school? I asked. Jimmy shrugged and walked away. I would have liked an answer—Tim Byrne had already invited me over—but I didn't push it. And Jimmy was waiting on the steps after the bell rang. We walked home without talking and then watched *Rocketship Seven* without talking and then he said, See you, and left.

For days I kept thinking I'd done something wrong. As if the list had been my idea. As if I could have told Father Murray his thinking exercise was stupid. Nellie Parker didn't help by being sick for another week. (I had to talk to her. Honest, I did.) Mom didn't help either by wondering if Timothy-the-turtle *was* okay out in the rockery. Didn't you bring the turtle in, Moo? asked Dad after the first storm in December. I thought you had, she answered. We searched and searched, brushing away snow with a broom, but he had vanished. Dad figured Timothy had dug under the frost line to stay warm. He'll crawl back out in April, he said. Hungry but happy. Ready to race the hare. Now, with winter ending, Mom was talking more and more about the turtle. I hope we didn't make a mistake, she kept saying. I'd feel just awful.

I felt just awful, or maybe just weird, after hearing some words spoken in our dining room. My parents were having a grown-ups party. Even though we kids had to eat in the kitchen before, I still liked these nights. The tablecloth and drippy candles. The folded napkins and fragile glasses. Adults ran wet fingers along the rims of the glasses to make them sing. Adults dangled spoons off their noses. Adults also talked and laughed and laughed and talked some more.

I loved listening. I loved pretending I was one of them. My secret spot—beneath the table, knees tucked under my chin—meant I couldn't see faces. Only voices. Only words. That night, six adult friends, mostly lumberjacks, rang the doorbell. Dad had to add an extra piece to the table, meaning you couldn't tip your chair back without hitting a wall. Six guests, two parents: eight bodies, sixteen legs. Now that I was ten, I didn't fit in the spot anymore. Even with my body a cocoon. Even with my head bowed. I crawled between Dad and Jack Pierce without their noticing. Dad found out quick and tickled me with his toes. Jack Pierce said that kids in the Foran house aren't seen or heard, only *felt*, and everyone laughed. (Strange: I suddenly thought of Elizabeth in our basement. Next time she visited, I'd definitely be nicer to her.) From my spot I could see Dad's arm lining wine bottles along the cupboard, and notice peoples' toes curling when they laughed or jerking back when Jack Pierce banged the table with his hand. Forks rattled and cups clinked. Candle flames jumped.

When Mr. So-and-So from Dad's office announced that he knew a good joke, everyone stopped talking. He began to speak in a funny accent, full of *zz* sounds and words in another language (not French). The joke didn't take long and, once it was over, the room was quiet. Then Dad sat back—his chair squeaks—and said, Good one, Bill. Mom offered more coffee. Her feet hid up under her chair, like a scared animal. The silence stretched out. Had they all drunk a magic potion and fallen asleep? Were they whispering about me? Come out, Charlie, Mom finally said. It's past your bedtime.

I had to say good night to the guests. For some reason I kept my eyes lowered; for some reason I was ashamed. In my room I repeated the joke in my head. I still didn't understand it, though, and I wound up dreaming about flying lambs that turned into jet bombers and furnaces that breathed fire.

I'm better today. Not so anxious. Not so confused. Dig yourself out, Timothy! (No bomb shelter under our . . .) Keep alive, Cousin Elizabeth in Blind River! (Mom said that Grandma, who I haven't seen in ages, can't visit us at Easter. Debbie may go stay with her . . .) Don't worry if kids make jokes about you, Nellie Parker! (If Father Ferguson had been the priest last Friday, instead of Father Larry, I'd have mentioned the joke. *Ze commandant callz together all ze Jews in ze camp . . .*) Forget about the thinking exercise, Jimmy! (Why did Jimmy Reilly throw the clock out the window? . . . *I haff zome good news and zome bad news. Ein, ze good news: you are all goink to Franz!* . . .) Forget about Adidas Rom and hockey too! (To see if time flies . . . *Yea! shouted ze prisoners. Zwei, said ze commandant, ze bad news . . .*) Know why? (Get it? Time flies! . . . *As zoap!*) Father Larry knows. (Going to Franz as zoap??) Because it's a new day. (INRI???) A new day on its way.

There it is too—my red balloon. Over near the crucifix: up above the organ pipes. How beautiful it is. How free. How safe as well, inside the church sky. Away from hunters. Away from winter.

We are all his children.

Charles Foran

Diary of a Cat (Part 3)

Hi everyone. "Wow," am I freezing. Snow isn't the same for a cat, you know. A snow pile to a kid is a mountain to me. Maybe a boy watches a storm from his window and thinks it's pretty. A cat gets stuck in it and thinks he'll die.

Sorry I sprayed the Forans furnitur last fall. Sorry I fought Tigger. Sorry also that I started to cling to the back screen door, run—ru-inn-ing it with my claws. I was hungry. And I was your cat—Pascal, the droolur.

Now I cling to the screen late at night and make it rattle, rattle. The okay boy, Charlie, hears me from his bedroom upstairs. He thinks the rattle is a bad dream. He feels responsibil. Being the only one up at night is scary, even when youre 10. The wind goes whooo. The furnace goes thrum. Rattle, rattle, hears Charlie. Poor Pascal. He must be so cold!

The boy turns on the porch light and opens the door. The glass is foggy. (His dad took off the ripped screen. "We'll buy a new one in the spring," he said.) The air bites his legs and slaps his face. Still, he stands there and looks into the dark. Does he see kitty prints? Maybe. Does he hear me cry? Maybe. Please come closer, Pascal, he begs. Please come into the light.

May

Bless me, Father, for I have sinned. It has been four weeks since my last confession . . . And I'm really glad it's you today, Father Ferguson. (The Grandma Ruthie smell gives him away.)

Who am I?

What?

Why does it matter if I am one priest or another? We are intermediaries. Your dialogue is with God.

I guess so, I say. Then, surprising myself, I sigh.

Well, isn't it?

How can I talk to God when he never answers?

People spend their lives learning how to speak with the Lord. You are just beginning to address the silence.

But I can talk to you right now, I say. And I know you are listening and will probably answer me. That's better. More . . . interesting, I guess.

Dear, oh dear, says Father Ferguson.

Sorry.

Please proceed.

Since then I have . . . I tell him some boring stuff.

Nothing a little more . . . urgent? he asks once I've finished.

LIKE, JIMMY HATES ME BECAUSE OF THE STUPID THING I SAID TO HIM? LIKE, I TOLD MOM AND DAD I DON'T WANT TO GO TO BLIND RIVER THIS SUMMER BECAUSE IT'S BORING, EVEN THOUGH IT'S BECAUSE I'M AFRAID MY COUSIN ELIZABETH WILL DIE WHILE I'M THERE? LIKE, I WAS RELIEVED WHEN THE ALTAR BOY CLASSES WERE CANCELLED, SO I WOULDN'T HAVE TO WEAR AN ANGEL DRESS? LIKE, I LET TIMOTHY-THE-TURTLE FREEZE TO DEATH?

I'm sorry about the way kids treat Nellie Parker, I add. It makes me feel awful.

Why?

She doesn't deserve it.

Have you treated her any better?

Yes.

Tried talking to her?

Yes. (Liar, liar!)

I understand she has stopped attending classes again. Is this true?

Sticks and stones won't break my bones, I say to myself, *but words will surely hurt me*. She stopped coming two weeks ago, I admit.

The cruelty of children, he says with a groan. A sobering reminder.

Of what?

He is silent.

Also, I did something incredibly terrible, I decide to say. (*No way I'll tell the priest about this*, I promised myself before opening the curtain.) A huge sin. Maybe one that can't be forgiven.

God forgives all who are genuinely penitent.

I tried to call the devil, Father.

Come again?

To talk with him. The way I'd talk with God.

Father Ferguson snorts. How, er, did you attempt to contact Satan?

The same way I do with God. On my knees beside the bed. Only, since I was calling hell, I hung upside-down with my head on the floor.

Was that comfortable?

Not very.

I bet, he says, snorting again. And tell me, did the devil answer your upside-down prayer?

Nope.

Pity, he says. Just as a matter of interest, what would you have asked him?

What happens to the soul of a boy who says and does evil things? I almost reply. But that would mean explaining to the priest what I said and did: not a smart idea. I don't know, I answer. Maybe just if, you know, he exists.

He does. Most certainly.

But the other priests—

Never mind them. Never mind—

There is a knock on the door. Father Ferguson says, Excuse me a moment. *Whack!* goes the window behind the screen. Voices start to murmur. Sweat starts to sting my eyes.

No one knows it, but I gave myself the last ear infection. For two nights running I lay in the bathtub listening to the drip of the tap and humming songs from the folk mass. On the third day, my ear closed. In my head there wasn't a seashell sound: this time, it was a raging river trapped between high rock walls and barrelling towards Niagara Falls. Boy, did it rage. Boy, was it barrelling. Doctor Cohen examined me with his flashlight. This infection is even deeper inside the canal, he told Mom. It could take a while.

What did I do for five days? Lie motionless until I left my body again and surfed the air? Pretend I was making Nellie Parker smile by telling her jokes and convincing her that everyone liked her, wanted her to come back? Mom borrowed more library books for me. I read one until the words started to blur: *The Singing Cave*, by Eilis Dillon, who lives in Ireland. (A kid up the street, Allan, moved there years ago. Pete Nicolson, who I still remember, lives in Paris.) The story is about a boy named Pat who stays with his grandfather on an island. One day he hears music from a cave beneath a cliff. You can only enter the cave from the ocean, so he and his grandfather row a boat out to it. Inside are stone bars that make music when the wind passes through them. Further in, way under the earth, is the skeleton of a Viking warrior. The Viking holds a sword and leans against the bow of a ship. Next to him is a chess set. What is a skeleton doing in an Irish cave? How come no one has found it before? The adventure begins.

When I couldn't read *The Singing Cave*, I stared at the cover. The drawing of the cave, and of Pat crouched inside it with a torch, reminded me of things. The walls were round and the floor was sand. Light was dim but not dark. You could imagine a train charging around a corner. You could imagine dwarfs marching in. You could also imagine a girl and a boy standing in a shallow sea, K-I-S-S-I-N-G. With another boy watching. His pants growing a bulge.

Jimmy came over to tell me about the final hockey game of the season. We won, eight to six, and he said he played okay, though my gloves and stick didn't help. Did time fly? I asked him. Mike, who slept downstairs while I was sick, said I could let his gerbil run under my sheets, if I wanted. Tell me a story about being in Grade One, I asked him. But then I interrupted with a tale about the day Jimmy and I got trapped in an old freezer. Kids die in those things, you know, I said to my brother. Debbie brought up her record player and put on the song "Sugar, Sugar," which was great, and "Light My Fire," which was awful. *Oh honey honey,* I sang to her, the music hurting my head.

I dreamed every night. I dreamed—

The slot opens. Sorry, says Father Ferguson, his voice a jolt. An unforeseen complication. Can you hold on a short while longer?

It's kind of—

Won't be more than a minute.

Whack!

I'm in darkness again. Sweating and stinking. Trying not to think about my back and knees. Trying to hum "Sugar, Sugar" but winding up stuck on some old French song: *Sur le pont d'Avignon* . . .

You're the one with my name, aren't you? said Grandpa in the dream. I'm Pat, I answered. We live in a singing cave together. Nonsense, he said. You can't fight the Krauts with a bar of soap. On a smoky battlefield—They got me, Sarge!—was a body in a *robe de chambre.* Is that you, Grandma? I asked. It's me, answered Nellie Parker, floating up over herself, her face and hair bloody. Don't you know that British Bulldog is forbidden? But you are my candy girl, I said to her. *I don't remember saying you could borrow my dressing gown,* answered Grandma. Nonsense, added Cousin Elizabeth. A bus driver isn't essential.

Worst of all, I can't see the red balloon. Can't watch it

soar in the sky. Can't relax and say, Whatever else is happening, at least I know the balloon is still out there. No wonder I could never be an altar boy. Jimmy wanted to be one—*Very* much so, he told me when Father Arnot announced that he was cancelling the class, since Father Larry had left the congregation unexpectedly—and he said my excuse about the white dress was stupid. How could I tell him the real reasons? That *I* caused Timothy's death—we found the shell a few days ago—and *I* let Coach Byrne make me number one goalie and *I* lied to get the hobby badge and *I* wanted to be Cub of the Year? How could I? Then I said those things. I knew what they meant: I was in control of my thoughts and my words. What, I asked Jimmy, are you *still* trying to become an angel? He shrugged, as usual. Your dad is Blue Collar, isn't he? I added, angry at him. So? he answered. So that means he's unskilled. It means he's working class. Jimmy blushed. (Get him upset and a freckle switch goes on.) What's working class? he asked. It means not like my dad, I answered. Not like most dads in the school. That's stupid, he said. It's true, I replied. Totally stupid, he repeated and turned away. Where are you going? I asked. Home, he said. Well, *I'm* going to Tim Byrne's house, I said. As if I care, answered Jimmy. As if I give a shit.

Grade Five boys don't give a shit. In the change room I realize how different our bodies are now. More bones and gangly limbs. Less fat and softness. Grade Five boys punch and kick and hope to draw blood in fights. Most have stopped biting, because that's how kids fight each other.

Grade Fives do it in an adult way. Same goes for language. Don't call someone a suck or a spaz. Call him a fairy or a faggot. Call her a witch or a cunt. Spell it out on the board: NELLIE PARKER SUCKS DOG COCKS.

My knees and back are screaming. *Sur le pont . . .* I worry I may fall backwards . . . *d'Avignon . . .* I wonder if I've given myself another ear infection . . . *On y danse . . .* I need out of here . . . *On y danse . . .* I need out, quic—

Whack!

Sorry to be so long, says Father Ferguson.

It's okay, I answer weakly.

Where were we?

I can't remember.

Just having a heart to heart, I imagine.

Should I tell you more sins?

Don't tell me, son. Tell . . . He stops and shifts in his seat. Would you do me one favour?

Sure.

Would you try not to pick at the skin around your thumbnails so much?

Did God ask you to say that?

No, your mother.

Oh.

She says you pick at them until they bleed.

I don't mean to.

I'm sure not.

I don't even know I'm—

Of course, says the priest.

We are both silent.

You asleep, son?

No.

Awake?

Yes.

Then start . . .

Finish, you mean?

For these and all . . .

For these and all my sins, I am heartily sorry.

As penance, I'd like you to say six Our Fathers, six Hail Marys and four Glory Bes. Don't be staring off into space while you pray, either. Concentrate.

That's a lot of penance, I say boldly. Were my sins so bad?

Not yours alone.

Okay.

Father Ferguson raises his right hand. I do too. Your part first, he says. I want to hear every word.

O my God, I begin, *I am heartily sorry for having offended thee. And I detest my sins above every other evil because they displease thee, my God, who art so deserving of all my love. And I firmly promise . . . umm . . . promise by thy holy grace never more to offend thee and to, uh, to amend my life.*

Excellent, he says. *God, the Father of mercy, reconciled the world to himself through the death and resurrection of his Son and gave the Holy Spirit in adundance for the forgiveness of sins. May he grant you pardon and peace through the ministry of the Church. And I absolve you from your sins in the name of the Father, and of the Son, and of the Holy Spirit.*

Amen, I say, making the sign of the cross.

Amen.

I stand. *Click* goes the light. You know, Father, I add, rubbing my knees, I already have a father. And a grandfather. You must too.

Go in peace, son.

Thanks.

Diary of a Cat (Final)

Remember purring Pascal? Remember the droolur? Maybe I found some other family to let me in during the winter. Maybe I'm fat and warm and sprayeing peoples furnitur over on Dunforest. But maybe I'm dead in your yard. That boy Charlie checked. In the shed. In the bushes. I saw him. I saw his face. It was winter for months and months. I had no food. I had no place to live. I saw him look. I saw his face.

Don't forget me, okay?

ACKNOWLEDGEMENTS

I am grateful to my editor, Iris Tupholme, for the notion that I should write such a book, and for her unflagging support of the project, even as it grew curiouser and curiouser. Ken Whyte at *Saturday Night* welcomed pieces of the manuscript into the magazine, while Dianne de Fenoyl and Dianna Symonds helped trim and polish them. My agent, Jan Whitford, of Westwood Creative Artists, was an excellent reader, as were David Manicom and Peter Petrasek. Other friends, too numerous to mention, listened patiently as I made adult sense of the narrative in conversation in order to make better kid sense of it on the page. On a practical note, I owe thanks to Heather Avery at Catherine Parr Traill College, Trent University, for the use of an office for a summer. On a bookish note, I found the Gessell Institute of Child Development series on childhood most helpful. Their guides kept my own development lines reasonably straight.

Mary Ladky let me read the manuscript to her and tried to laugh on cue. Anna and Claire, our daughters, gave silent assent to my pilfering of their words, actions and—it is hoped—their imaginations. No exaggeration here: they made *The Story of My Life (so far)* possible.

My sister, Debbie Foran-Makarenko, was both a clear-eyed companion three decades into the past and a tolerant subject of my purposeful character sketchings. Her sons, Matthew, Sean and Mark, helped out more than they knew, and my brother, Mike Foran, remembered some good stuff. Muriel Foran kept the 1971 school assignment that lends the book its title. Both my parents were generous with their time and, needless to say, their/our lives. No exaggeration here again: they made *The Story of My Life (so far)* possible.

Finally, Jim Russell conjured our shared history with greater acuity, honesty and humour than I could have mustered on my own. I was delighted to call him my bestest best friend in 1968; I happily still call him that today.

How much of this story is recollection and how much of it is imagined? Even at age ten, it appears that I was already forgetting details of my earlier self and busy recasting the past to suit an understanding, perhaps a yearning, tailored to my needs. Logically, the childhood offered here must also be at the mercy of current exigencies.

That I seem to remember so vividly my earliest encounters with my cousin Elizabeth, for example, who returned to our house several times in the years following this narrative in her losing battle with a brain tumour, is perhaps a function of my now being a parent. All of us, I suspect, are always the sum of the ongoing interplay between our recollections (not to mention forgettings) and our dreams and visions (not to mention nightmares). Thus exists, for perpetuity, a protean, eternal childhood self, as oblivious to the rules of memory as to the vicissitudes of time.